Cash Flow and Performance Measurement: Managing for Value

by Henry A. Davis

A publication of Financial Executives Research Foundation, Inc.

658.15
D263c

HF
5681
.C28
D38
1996

Kelso

Financial Executives Research Foundation, Inc.
10 Madison Avenue, Box 1938
Morristown, New Jersey 07962-1938
(973) 898-4608

Copyright © 1996 by Financial Executives Research Foundation, Inc.

All rights reserved. No part of this book may be reproduced in any form or by any means without written permission from the publisher.

International Standard Book Number 1-885065-07-8
Library of Congress Catalog Card Number 95-83616
Printed in the United States of America

Second Printing

Financial Executives Research Foundation, Inc. (FERF®) is the research affiliate of Financial Executives Institute. The basic purpose of the Foundation is to sponsor research and publish informative material in the field of business management, with particular emphasis on the practice of financial management and its evolving role in the management of business.

The views set forth in this publication are those of the author and do not necessarily represent those of the FERF Board as a whole, individual trustees, or the members of the Project Advisory Committee.

FERF publications can be ordered by calling 1-800-680-FERF (U.S. and Canada only; international orders, please call 770-751-1986). Quantity discounts are available.

Project Advisory Committee

A. Douglas Hartt (Chairman)
Treasurer
Maritime Tel. & Tel. Co. Ltd.

Charles W. Cantwell
Manager, Special Studies—Packaging and Industrial Polymers
E. I. du Pont de Nemours and Co.

Paul S. Gifford
Director—Investor Relations
The Boeing Company

J. James Lewis
Executive Vice President
Financial Executives Research Foundation, Inc.

Arthur V. Neis
Treasurer & CFO
Life Care Services Corporation

William M. Sinnett
Senior Research Associate
Financial Executives Research Foundation, Inc.

John W. van Dyke
Senior Vice President and Chief Financial Officer
American Optical Corporation

Janet F. Hastie
Director of Communications
Financial Executives Research Foundation, Inc.

University Libraries
Carnegie Mellon University
Pittsburgh, PA 15213-3890

Contents

Introduction   1

1   Summary   5
Performance Measures Used   5
    Case-Study Company Preferences   5
    Mail Survey Results   6
Implementing Financial Performance Measures   7
Overview of Case-Study Companies   9

2   How Companies Use Performance Measures   18
A Comparison of Two of the Newer Measurement
Systems   19
    Economic Value Added   19
    Cash Flow Return on Investment   20
Utilization of Performance Measures   23
    Case-Study Companies   23
    Mail Survey Respondents   25
Other Measurement-Related Issues   27
    Continued Use of Traditional Measures   27
    Replacement of Unsuitable Metrics   28
    More Attention to the Balance Sheet   28
    Separation of Investment Decisions from
    Financing Decisions   28
    Use of Both Operating and Nonfinancial
    Performance Measures   29
    Adaptation of Measures to Each Business   30

3   How Companies Select and Implement Performance
Measures   31
Decision Making   33
    Effect on Management   33
    Delegation of Decision-Making and Spending
    Authority   33
The Role of the Finance Function in Performance
Measurement   34
    Effect of Measurement Systems on Financial
    Structure/Strategy   35

Internal Financial Reporting Systems 35
Explaining Performance Measures 35
Evaluation and Compensation of Management 36
Conflict Between Short- and Long-term Measures 39
Calculation of Amount of Capital
Invested in Businesses 39
Adjustments to Earnings and Capital Invested 41
Capitalized Research and Development Expenses 43

4 How Shareholder Value Is Created 47
Investors' Objectives 47
Valuation Methods 48
Correlation of Performance Measures to
Shareholder Value 50
How Financial Risk Management Relates to Valuation 51

5 How Capital Budgeting Decisions Are Related to
Performance Management 52
Procedure for Submitting Proposals 54
Financial and Nonfinancial Considerations 54
Cost of Capital and Hurdle Rates 54
Intangibles in Capital Budgeting Analysis 57
Asset or Real Options 58
Decision Trees and Probability Analysis 59

6 American Optical Corporation 62

7 AT&T Corp. 69

8 The Boeing Company 78

9 The Clorox Company 88

10 E.I. du Pont de Nemours and Co. 98

11 Federal Signal Corporation 112

12 FMC Corporation   121

13 Meredith Corporation   131

14 National Semiconductor Corporation   140

15 PepsiCo, Inc.   159

16 Pioneer Hi-Bred International, Inc.   170

17 Simon Property Group, Inc.   181

Appendices

A Survey Results   193

B Survey Respondents by Industry   201

C Interview Protocol   203

Bibliography   207

Glossary   211

About the Author   218

Acknowledgments   219

Introduction

The managements of many companies, in today's economic environment, are focusing on the creation of shareholder value as their fundamental goal, rather than just sales and earnings growth. In this regard, they have identified and developed financial performance measures to evaluate their business units and managers for the purpose of increasing shareholder value.

This research project documents the financial performance measures used by a representative group of companies and describes how the measures were selected, how they are used to measure business-unit performance, and how they are used to evaluate and compensate management. The project also focuses on how **capital budgeting**,[1] performance measurement, and valuation methods are coordinated.

For this project, 12 companies were interviewed on site and used as a basis for case studies. The companies were selected to represent a range of industries and revenue levels and to illustrate the use of a variety of well-known financial performance measures. Questions were designed to explore what performance measures are used, why they were selected, and how they have been implemented. Several persons from each company were interviewed. Interviews were conducted one-on-one and in groups; follow-up interviews were conducted with each company by telephone.

Based on the case studies, a mail survey was developed to compare the interview findings across a large number of companies. The questions, mostly multiple choice, were designed to obtain definitive answers suitable for tabulation. Some questions required a brief written response: for example, respondents were asked to specify the **discount rate** used for capital budgeting and any performance measures used that were not already listed in the survey.

This mail survey was sent to members of Financial Executives Institute (FEI) from 450 companies representing a broad range of industries in the United States and Canada. One hundred and fifty-three responses (34 percent) were received. Twenty-two of the companies responding were interviewed by telephone. These interviews helped the researcher

---

[1] Terms explained in the glossary are boldfaced on first reference throughout the text.

1

interpret the survey results and further explore topics covered with the case-study companies.

How to Use This Book

Chapter 1 provides the report's principal findings. Chapter 2 describes performance measures used by the case-study companies and the mail survey respondents. Chapter 3 explains how case-study companies have selected and implemented their performance measures. Chapter 4 details how the companies have defined investors' objectives and developed their own valuation methods. Chapter 5 describes how companies have coordinated valuation and performance measurement with their capital budgeting procedures. Chapters 6 through 17 contain the case studies.

Appendix A includes the questions asked and results of the mail survey. Appendix B lists the industries of the mail survey respondents. Appendix C contains the protocol used for interviews with the case-study companies.

The glossary explains a number of technical terms used in the study, and the bibliography lists a few well-known reference books on financial performance measures, capital budgeting, and corporate valuation.

For the convenience of the reader, the brief glossary that follows defines abbreviations and acronyms for technical terms used in this book.

Glossary of Abbreviations and Acronyms

ATOI	after-tax operating income
CAGR	cumulative annual revenue growth rate
CAPM	capital asset pricing model
CFROI	cash flow return on investment
CVM	Clorox Value Measure
DCF	discounted cash flow
EBIT	earnings before interest and taxes
EBITDA	earnings before interest, income taxes, depreciation, and amortization
EPS	earnings per share
FAD	funds available for distribution

FFO	funds from operations
FIFO	first-in, first-out inventory accounting
GAAP	generally accepted accounting principles
IRR	internal rate of return
LIFO	last-in, first-out inventory accounting
NOPAT	net operating profit after taxes
NPV	net present value
NSVM	National Semiconductor Value Model
REIT	real estate investment trust
R&D	research and development
ROA	return on assets
ROE	return on equity, return on common equity
ROI	return on investment
RONA	return on net assets
SBU	strategic business unit
SCFROI	sustainable cash flow return on investment
SVA	Shareholder Value Analysis (as used by Boeing)
	shareholder value added (as used by DuPont)
TSR	total shareholder return
WACC	weighted average cost of capital

1

Summary

Interviews with executives at 12 case-study companies revealed that while the executives of these companies used different financial performance measures, all were concerned with creating shareholder value by generating earnings and cash flow greater than the cost of the capital entrusted to them.

Performance Measures Used

The results of the case-study interviews and the responses to the survey are the basis of the principal findings of this study. The case-study interviews identified a series of steps that companies can follow to implement performance measures to increase shareholder value.

Case-Study Company Preferences

The case-study companies use both **earnings-based** and **cash-flow-based performance measures** to evaluate the performance of business units and managers.

- ☐ Of the twelve companies, five use primarily earnings-based measures, two use primarily cash-flow-based measures, and five use a combination of earnings-based and cash-flow-based measures.

- ☐ Five companies use **economic value added**, an earnings-based measure, as one of their principal performance measures, and one is considering it.

- ☐ Two of the companies that use primarily earnings-based measures believe that their earnings and cash flow track closely over time.

5

□ Of the companies that use cash-flow-based measures, one uses an internal **discounted cash flow** (DCF) valuation model, and one uses the proprietary **cash flow return on investment** (CFROI) model.

□ The companies that use earnings-based performance measures generally believe that those measures are more effective for shorter periods, such as one year, and that cash-flow measures are more effective for longer periods.

□ The companies that use earnings-based performance measures continue to use DCF analysis for capital budgeting and corporate valuation.

Mail Survey Results

The complete mail survey results can be found in Appendix A. Consistent with the case-study companies, most companies responding to the survey mentioned several financial performance measures that are used for at least part of management compensation. Given a list of nine performance measures, companies were asked to check all that they use and add others if applicable.

□ Of the 153 companies that responded, the majority (66.0 percent) reported that they use more than two financial performance measures, 34 (22.2 percent) use two measures, and 18 (11.8 percent) use one performance measure.

□ A total of 40 companies (26.1 percent) noted that they use economic value added, either alone or in combination with other performance measures.

□ A total of 32 companies (20.9 percent) use CFROI either alone or in combination with other performance measures.

It is interesting to note that 70 companies (45.8 percent) responding to the survey believe that **free cash flow** has a stronger effect on their share price, compared with 72 companies (47.1 percent) who believe that their share price is influenced more by net income.

Analysis of the survey results also shows that traditional financial performance measures continue to be widely used. Operating earnings was the measure most frequently cited (111 companies or 72.5 percent), although only five companies mentioned using this measure exclusively.

Implementing Financial Performance Measures

Although the case-study companies have adopted a variety of financial performance measures appropriate to their individual business needs, their collective experience provides a number of basic steps that companies should consider when selecting and implementing measures to increase shareholder value.

1. **Establish the process.**
   □ Obtain commitment and agreement among top management and the board of directors on the principal ways the company is valued by investors and how the company's strategic plan is coordinated with its plan to create shareholder value.
   □ Involve managers at all levels in the design of their own performance measures, including ones that relate directly and indirectly to the creation of shareholder value.
   □ Develop a valuation model that managers can use to estimate the effect of various strategies, scenarios, and assumptions on shareholder value.

2. **Promote understanding.**
   □ Assist managers and employees throughout the company in understanding the basics of corporate finance and how their jobs and their performance measures relate to the creation of shareholder value.
   □ Ensure that performance measures are understood at each level and give clear signals for management decision making.
   □ Make shareholders aware of investments that may restrict earnings in the short term but create value over the longer term.

3. **Motivate managers.**
   □ Align management incentives with the goals of the business. Help managers to understand performance measures in the context of broader business goals.

☐ Give managers incentives for both growth and returns above the **cost of capital**.

☐ Tie performance measures to compensation.

☐ Base bonuses on more than one year's performance and develop deferred bonus plans to encourage a long-term perspective.

☐ Eliminate upper limits on bonuses, or at least make the threshold high enough to encourage managers to act like entrepreneurs.

☐ Design compensation and savings incentive programs to encourage employees to own company stock and understand factors that drive its price.

4. **Monitor the process.**
   ☐ Use performance measures consistently over time, but also revise measures selectively as conditions and objectives change.

   ☐ Periodically compare an internal corporate valuation with the company's actual market value, and analyze the reasons for any difference.

5. **Avoid common pitfalls.**
   ☐ Ensure that performance measures do not confuse operating performance with financing decisions. The decision to invest in a project should be made first; how to finance the project should be a separate decision.

   ☐ Recognize that no single measure suits all purposes.

   ☐ Evaluate the trade-off between accuracy and complexity.

   ☐ Use a balanced scorecard of multiple performance measures.

   ☐ Guard against investment decisions that produce short-term results at the expense of creating long-term value.

Overview of Case-Study Companies

Results of the company interviews are presented beginning with Chapter 6. Following are highlights of the findings at each of the companies interviewed.

American Optical Corporation

American Optical is a diversified manufacturer whose products include lenses, bonded abrasives, and steel tubing. The company requires a minimum of three performance measures for each division: economic value added, **return on net assets** (RONA), and free cash flow. Management believes that minimum return targets and a standard measure such as economic value added for quantifying change offer an objective approach to performance evaluation. Economic value added provides a standard measure that makes managers' goals clear and consistent and prevents managers from making excuses for poor performance or emphasizing other measures disproportionately. RONA provides a useful measure of operating performance that excludes financing considerations. Free cash flow reminds managers that cash flow underlies the value of their businesses. Business-unit managers also recommend other measures, which are negotiated and approved at the corporate level. Operating performance measures such as revenue per employee are used as benchmarks for improving the productivity of manufacturing operations.

The company's compensation formula includes both economic value added for the year and the change in economic value added from the previous year. Bonuses have current and deferred portions and no upper limits; they encourage managers to make investment commitments that will produce rewards in future years even if near-term results are penalized.

Capital investment requests include the calculation of **internal rate of return** (IRR), economic value added, and **payback**. The company favors projects with payback periods of two years or less.

AT&T Corp.

AT&T believes that top management commitment and a link to compensation are required for a performance measurement system to be effective. The company uses economic value added in addition to monthly and quarterly operating income to measure business managers' performance. Economic value added was adopted shortly after the company was reorganized into strategic business units (SBUs). Measured operating income, adopted in the mid-1980s, was easy to apply across many diverse businesses, but it did not account for cash flow or reflect business-unit balance sheets. AT&T needed a measure that represents shareholders' interests, eliminates accounting biases, can be applied throughout the business planning process from 10-year business plans to plan/actual reviews during the budget year, and gives management appropriate incentives for action. To implement economic value added, AT&T aligned a balance sheet with each SBU, developed a chart of accounts, and redesigned its internal management reporting system to convert statements prepared according to generally accepted accounting principles (GAAP). Economic value added has given all managers a uniform, simple measure of what the company thinks will enhance shareholder value. Because a business unit's economic value added is not affected by the method of financing, the measure has helped separate business and financing decisions.

While economic value added is used for planning, budgeting, and performance measurement, DCF analysis is still used for project evaluation and decision making. AT&T uses a uniform cost of capital across all nonfinancial business units for capital budgeting and makes adjustments for projects of higher-than-normal risk.

The Boeing Company

Boeing, the aerospace company, recently implemented its Shareholder Value Analysis (SVA) plan, in which it calculates its own share value based on projected cash flows in a long-term plan discounted at its **weighted average cost of capital** (WACC). Boeing's management believes that its cash-flow-based valuation and performance measurement program is better aligned with the creation of shareholder value and better understood by its managers than the accounting-based method it used in the past.

Incentive compensation is based on how well executives have met their parts of the plan and how the actual market value of the company's stock compares with its expected value. For top executives, incentive compensation is based on both increased shareholder value and measures that include quality as determined by customer, employee, and community satisfaction. For executives in product groups, incentive compensation is based on company, group, and individual performance. The primary group performance measures are profit contribution, unit cost, cycle time, and market share.

Boeing gathered evidence on the correlation of various metrics with market price per share and found that the correlation of price/earnings ratios and earnings per share (EPS) growth rates was poor, the correlation of **return on equity**[1] (ROE) minus the cost of capital was somewhat better, and the correlation of predicted value per share based on analysts' cash-flow forecasts was strong, even though there may be volatility over short periods. The ROE target the company had used in the past was based on accounting earnings, which were determined largely by the program method of accounting for aircraft production and were not a reliable measure of its economic performance. To implement SVA, Boeing has begun an education program to explain the fundamentals of DCF, **net present value** (NPV), and corporate valuation. Boeing believes that its value is best understood by institutional investors with a long-term perspective who base their analysis primarily on their estimates of future cash flows discounted at the company's WACC.

The Clorox Company

Clorox, a diversified consumer products company, developed its Clorox Value Measure (CVM), a variant of economic value added, to focus people in all functions on what creates shareholder value. The company wanted an operating measure that would correlate with shareholder return and relate NPV analysis of new investments with the evaluation of ongoing operations. In management's view, economic value added and CFROI were the best choices; CFROI appeared to have a higher correlation with shareholder value but was harder to explain to and implement with operating people.

Part of compensation for vice presidents, directors in SBUs, and senior managers is tied to CVM. The measure has helped managers identify trade-offs among growth, operating margin, and utilization of assets and improve the management of inventory, accounts receivable, and capital expenditures. Clorox utilized a board game to help explain CVM to non-

---

[1] For the purposes of this book, the terms **return on common equity** and *return on equity* are used interchangeably and are abbreviated as *ROE*.

financial managers and to make the learning process easy and enjoyable. The company's treasurer believes that investment decisions should be based on DCF. Financial managers caution that large investments will sometimes hurt economic value added in the short run and that managers have to be confident and patient enough to make decisions that will contribute to economic value added several years hence.

E.I. du Pont de Nemours and Co.

DuPont's principal financial metrics for evaluating business unit performance are after-tax operating income (ATOI) and components of cash flow not related to financing. Recently, the chemical company introduced two new financial performance measures, RONA and shareholder value added (SVA), a variant of economic value added. This change was partly motivated by a reorganization that delegated increased responsibility to SBUs and called for ways to measure the financial performance of those units as if they were independent businesses.

DuPont considers RONA an improvement over ROE as a profitability measure because it takes into account management of the entire balance sheet without consideration of external financing. SVA is a useful addition because it unites earnings and investment in a single monetary measure of performance. It makes managers more aware of the corporate resources they are using. How the general managers use performance measures beyond ATOI and cash flow within their SBUs is left to their discretion. DuPont believes that the SVA measure will be most helpful when it can be used to measure the progress of its businesses over time.

Federal Signal Corporation

Federal Signal is a diversified manufacturer whose products include fire engines, rescue vehicles, street-sweeping vehicles, industrial tools, and corporate signage. Federal Signal's two most important financial objectives are a 15 percent average increase in annual EPS over time and a 20 percent ROE. At the business-unit level, the ROE metric is effectively a RONA metric. Management considers the achievement of the company's financial goals to be rooted in basic operating performance, and it pays close attention to **operating margins**, working capital, and other asset utilization measures. It has used these performance measures for decades.

A large part of division presidents' compensation is based on how well they have carried out their strategic plans, how the performance of their businesses has improved over the past several years, how difficult their plans have been to achieve, and how well they have attended to key value-based measures such as sales growth. Recently, the company has begun using a matrix for certain operating groups that defines a bonus level for each combination of sales growth and operating margin. The matrix will help managers see how various growth and return targets create value, and it will add objectivity to the bonus plan.

With a DCF valuation model, Federal Signal's managers can compare the benefits to be gained from margin improvement, working capital reduction, and growth. In some cases, they have created value by reducing margins in order to grow. Federal Signal believes that its EPS growth and ROE metrics, continued focus on operating margins, working capital, and other asset utilization measures, and the DCF valuation model have helped its managers align their decisions with the creation of shareholder value.

FMC Corporation

FMC is a diversified manufacturing company whose products include industrial chemicals, machinery and equipment, defense systems, and precious metals. FMC adopted economic value added with relatively few adjustments because it is easy for business managers to understand. Also, each division develops a balanced scorecard of financial and non-financial measures that are approved at the corporate level. In the early 1980s, when the company was more diversified, it used the CFROI model as part of an analytic process to rationalize its portfolio of businesses, but the model was difficult to implement in the business units. It was based on a complex IRR model rather than the traditional profit-and-loss model with which managers were familiar. FMC uses managers' estimates of economic value added over a three-year time period as a basis for incentive compensation. Division managers can increase their bonuses by defining and achieving "stretch" targets.

FMC's controller believes that the new measurement systems have changed FMC's culture in two important ways. First, they have moved the company away from using the annual budget as a basis for incentive compensation. Second, the use of nonfinancial measures in the balanced scorecard has made business managers think more broadly and strategically.

Meredith Corporation

Meredith is a magazine publishing and broadcasting company. In 1993, following a restructuring and downsizing, Meredith's management concluded that a 15 percent ROE was necessary to make it one of the top five companies in the media industry, and they developed a five-year plan to achieve that goal. The ROE metric and the company's plans for achieving it, business by business, have been good vehicles for teaching people about the company's financial objectives. They have provided an impetus for revenue growth and cost control in all of Meredith's businesses. Once current ROE goals are achieved, the company will consider a new, more complex measure such as economic value added.

Meredith has both long-term incentive plans tied to ROE and annual incentive plans tied to earnings and cash flow. Each group also uses additional measures important to its business, such as advertising revenues for magazines. The company is less discretionary than it used to be in determining its performance packages. If managers do not achieve defined target numbers, they do not receive bonuses.

Magazine publishing and broadcasting businesses are sometimes valued in different ways. Magazine publishers are valued based on revenues and earnings, though some analysts capitalize cash flows. Broadcast businesses are valued primarily on cash flow. Because Meredith is in both businesses, some analysts value those businesses separately and compute a **break-up value**.

National Semiconductor Corporation

National Semiconductor recently began to use a model it calls the National Semiconductor Value Model (NSVM), based on CFROI, to better align its strategic planning with the creation of shareholder value. CFROI is an IRR measure that equates the current dollar gross investment with future cash flows and the eventual release of nondepreciating assets. Previous accounting-based performance measures and incentive plans were focused on the short term and did not correlate closely with the creation of shareholder value. RONA was a useful interim measure that helped divisions focus on their balance sheets.

CFROI has helped divisions justify investments in new plants and equipment in an industry where growth is required for survival. It helps the company avoid the "old plant–new plant" trap, frequently found with RONA, in which returns on depreciated assets appear to be relatively high, and new capital investments are difficult to justify because they reflect lower returns in the first few years. The CFROI model is used by the top few people in each division for strategic planning and investment decision making. Other managers are measured by more traditional metrics.

PepsiCo, Inc.

PepsiCo, the beverage, snack food, and restaurant company, uses a full range of traditional financial performance measures. In its annual report, PepsiCo describes four metrics: volume growth, operating profit growth, cash growth, and investment returns above the company's WACC. PepsiCo believes that the measures it uses are as effective as any of the well-known, value-based measures. Management believes that improved performance over time using consistent measures is more important than the actual measures used. Despite the increasing importance management is placing on cash flow, PepsiCo still believes it is important to meet its objectives and deliver consistent growth in quarterly EPS. If quarterly EPS growth starts to lag behind its historic rates, analysts can be expected to reduce their long-term growth estimates accordingly.

PepsiCo has a **hurdle rate** for investments that is above its WACC and higher hurdle rates for developing countries. While the company tries to manage so that cash flow and earnings grow at about the same rate, it recognizes that some international businesses require net investments with negative cash flows for several years while markets are being developed. PepsiCo projects cash flows based on current strategies for each of its businesses. It values each business and then values the enterprise as a whole, comparing that value with the company's current market value.

Pioneer Hi-Bred International, Inc.

Pioneer Hi-Bred is a breeder and producer of corn and other hybrid and varietal seed products. Its principal metrics for business performance and management incentives are ROE and growth in EPS. Management adopted ROE in conjunction with a continuing focus on **return on assets**

(ROA) at the business-unit level because it was easy to explain throughout the company, and it could be used to promote the kind of behavior that would enhance shareholder value. The company is moving toward a balanced scorecard of financial and nonfinancial business-unit performance measures including customer satisfaction, product performance advantage, market share, and pricing in relation to value.

Long-term, value-based incentive plans are an important part of management's reward for performance. An award of restricted stock is based on earnings growth over a three-year period. Within divisions, functional measures that managers can influence are used (e.g., return on sales and growth in sales for sales managers; fixed and variable cost growth for plant managers). Each year, eligible employees share equally in a profit-sharing program regardless of their base pay, where they work, or what they do.

Research and development (R&D) is an important intangible asset, and managing R&D expenditures is a key part of Pioneer Hi-Bred's strategic planning, but it does not capitalize R&D expenses. The company has started an R&D management process in which it seeks a balance between quantitative analysis and qualitative and strategic considerations. It finds that the analysis of probabilities and ranges of possible outcomes is useful, but NPV analysis has limitations because of the uncertainty and time horizons of its research projects.

Simon Property Group, Inc.

Simon is a **real estate investment trust** (REIT). Its growth and profitability are based on its ability to maintain high occupancy in its malls, to develop an environment capable of producing high sales performance, to get the highest possible rent on new leases, and to control costs. The principal financial measures for Simon and other REITs are **funds from operations** (FFO), **earnings before interest, income taxes, depreciation, and amortization** (EBITDA), and **funds available for distribution** (FAD). FFO, a measure unique to the real estate industry, is calculated as net income from operating activities before considering the impact of depreciation and amortization of assets that are unique to real estate. REIT stocks are valued and compared by multiples of FFO. EBITDA is an industry standard used to compare REITs' operating performance before the effect of capital structure. FAD is calculated by subtracting operating capital expenditures from FFO. The company's dividend divided by FAD is referred to as the dividend payout ratio.

Simon has designed a performance measurement system to focus on the results shareholders expect. To determine incentive compensation for the vice presidents of management, leasing, and development in each region, it has developed a matrix that defines the percentage of a person's cash bonus that is determined by measures such as FFO, percentage occupancy, minimum rent, and specialty leasing income. A restricted stock incentive plan for vice presidents and above is based on FFO over a five-year period and vests over nine years. Simon believes that its performance measurement system encourages managers in the management, leasing, and development functions to work together and to focus on the operating and financial performance measures that reflect growth, profitability, and the creation of shareholder value.

2

How Companies Use
Performance Measures

An effective measurement system consists of a medley, or "balanced scorecard," of financial and nonfinancial performance measures tied to earnings, cash flow, and the creation of shareholder value. The case-study companies and mail survey respondents use a full range of traditional financial performance measures and newer measures tied to the creation of shareholder value. Traditional financial measures include operating earnings, ROE, **return on investment** (ROI), and ROA.

While continuing to use these traditional measures, companies also have recognized their limitations and developed new measures in recent years to provide better indicators of operating performance and shareholder value creation. RONA was developed as an improvement over ROE. RONA is net operating profit (that is, before financing charges) divided by net assets; net assets are defined as total assets minus non-interest-bearing liabilities. Whereas the ROE ratio can be influenced by the amount of a company's leverage, RONA is a measure of operating performance that is not influenced by the company's financial structure. **Total shareholder return** (TSR) was developed as a measure of both price appreciation and dividends. It assumes that all dividends are reinvested with the company to take earnings on dividends into account. Disclosure of TSR is now required by the Securities and Exchange Commission.

A Comparison of Two of the Newer Measurement Systems

Although performance measures such as ROA, RONA, and ROE are useful for comparing companies with one another and for analyzing a given company over time, they generally are not considered good indicators of a company's stock price. Companies have looked for measures that are better correlated with the creation of shareholder value to evaluate their business units and managers. Two of the best known value-based performance metrics used today are economic value added and CFROI. The following section compares their principal features.

Economic Value Added

Economic value added, or **economic profit**, is a measure of earnings minus a capital charge. Earnings for this metric are a company's accrual-based **net operating profit after taxes** (NOPAT) with some adjustments. The capital charge is based on the total capital invested in the company at book value, net of depreciation. It is generally considered to be equal to net assets, or total assets minus non-interest-bearing current liabilities. Economic value added can be considered the dollar value of RONA minus a capital charge. The capital charge is generally calculated as the WACC times capital invested. The **capital asset pricing model** (CAPM) is used to calculate the cost of equity. A number of adjustments can be made to both earnings and capital invested to produce the most accurate possible measure of economic profit. Operating leases and investments in intangibles such as R&D may be capitalized. Amortized goodwill, deferred taxes, items previously written off (such as restructured or discontinued operations), and other reserves may be added back to capital. Not writing off assets for restructured or discontinued operations is consistent with the philosophy of earning a return on every dollar invested. Managers are encouraged to make decisions that will improve earnings in the future and not to shy away from disposing of assets because of the effect that a write-off will have on their current earnings. The reversal of write-offs and other adjustments are explained in more detail in Chapter 3.

Economic value added, representing earnings above the company's cost of capital, is consistent with NPV calculated with the cost of capital as a discount rate. A company that consistently makes investments with a positive NPV will keep generating economic value added. NPV can be calculated using either DCF or discounted economic value added; the answers will be similar.

The case-study companies that use economic value added believe that such an accrual-based performance measurement system is well adapted to the evaluation of performance for a given year, whereas cash-flow-based evaluation is more effective for a longer period. Managers are evaluated based on economic value added and year-to-year improvement in economic value added. The objective of an economic-value-added measurement system is to maximize **market value added**, which is the difference between the company's market value and total **capital invested**.

Economic value added is easily understood because it is based on reported earnings according to the accrual accounting model. To the extent a company makes adjustments to earnings and capital invested to create a more accurate measure of economic profit, this metric may become more complicated. An important behavioral change that results from measuring economic value added is increased attention to the balance sheet and the cost of capital. Managers have a financial incentive to minimize working capital and to forego proposals for new plant and equipment that may have a greater impact on capital invested than on incremental earnings and economic value added. The capital charge for economic value added is based on book capital, net of depreciation. If not used properly, this metric may act as a disincentive for new investment at current prices, even when projected cash flows reflect a positive NPV over the life of a project.

Cash Flow Return on Investment

The CFROI metric is a proprietary model based on the premise that future cash flows can be projected based on a company's current performance, as measured by IRR. This includes adjustments for continuing new investment to renew and expand the capital base and for the gradual fading of above-average returns to market norms over time. According to the CFROI school of thought, few companies are able to earn returns substantially above market norms for sustained periods, and the market does not support a company stock price that anticipates excess returns.

CFROI is an IRR calculation that equates the current gross investment in the business with future cash flows and a residual value of nondepreciating assets. It is based on an assumption that most corporate projects are like annuities, earning relatively even returns until the end of their lives. Those projects are like an investment in an automobile, which delivers relatively consistent performance until repair bills start mounting up toward the end of its useful life. The CFROI of a company is equivalent to the IRR of all its individual projects, irrespective of the growth rate of the business.

CFROI can be calculated using either an IRR method or an algebraic method. The IRR calculation is based on (a) an initial investment, the gross investment in the business, (b) gross cash flows over the useful life of the company's assets, and (c) a future value at the end of the period comprised of working capital and nondepreciating assets. The shorter algebraic method calculates CFROI as operating income divided by net assets. In the calculation of operating income, rental expense is added back to operating income and book depreciation is replaced with economic depreciation. In the calculation of net assets, accumulated depreciation is added back, an inflation adjustment is made, and operating rental expenses are capitalized.

CFROI is a real measure, net of inflation, that should be compared with a real cost of capital. Gross investment is calculated in constant dollars, avoiding the "old plant–new plant" trap in which older, more depreciated assets show higher returns than newer and usually more productive assets purchased at current prices. Constant dollars are considered a less subjective measure for asset values than replacement costs and consistent with the investor's desire for a return in constant units of purchasing power.

The company's current CFROI is considered to be its normal level of performance. For corporate valuation, future cash flows are calculated starting with the current CFROI and adjusting year by year for increased gross investment and a fading of the company's returns to national corporate averages over time. (The model assumes that above- or below-average returns will gravitate toward national averages over time, and that the market will not pay for sustained above-average returns.) The resulting cash flows are discounted at a market-derived rate that is calculated based on the CFROIs, sustainable asset growth rates, and current market prices of the entire list of Standard & Poor's 500 Index companies. Managers are judged based on the current CFROI, the current corporate spot value using the CFROI model, and TSR. TSR is driven by three factors: (1) CFROI, the ability to maintain or increase profitability from an existing asset base; (2) growth, the ability to invest cash at returns above the cost of capital; and (3) discipline to harvest cash and pay dividends to shareholders when appropriate. Corporate users of the CFROI metric believe that it provides managers with the most accurate possible projections of performance resulting from their investment decisions and valuations that have the most accurate possible correlations with market prices. Table 2-1 compares the principal features of the economic value added and CFROI metrics.

TABLE 2-1 Comparison of Economic Value Added and Cash Flow
          Return on Investment Metrics

Economic Value Added	*Cash Flow Return on Investment*
Measurement: earnings minus capital charge.	**Measurement**: internal rate of return (IRR) that considers the whole company to be a project.
Capital Charge: based on historical capital invested, net of depreciation.	**Initial Investment for IRR Calculation**: based on gross investment in current dollars.
Corporate Valuation: requires estimation of future economic value added or future cash flows.	**Corporate Valuation**: future cash flows are estimated based on today's CFROI, an assumed growth in gross investment, and an assumed fade of above-average returns to market norms over time.
Discount Rate: weighted average cost of capital, using capital asset pricing model for equity cost component.	**Discount Rate**: derived from CFROI and market prices of Standard and Poor's 500 companies.
Evaluation of Managers: based on economic value added and year-to-year increase in economic value added. Ultimate objective is to maximize market value added, which is the difference between market value and the total amount invested by shareholders.	**Evaluation of Managers**: based on CFROI, corporate spot valuation using CFROI model, and total shareholder return, which is the IRR that equates today's spot value with cash flows generated in future years and the residual value of nondepreciating assets at the end of the period.
Ability to Be Understood: easy, because it is based on accrued earnings measured by the accounting model, but can be complex depending on the number of adjustments made to earnings and capital invested.	**Ability to Be Understood**: complex in the beginning until IRR logic is understood. Requires aggregate market data for calculation of fade rate and discount rate.

Utilization of Performance Measures

Case-Study Companies

The 12 case-study companies demonstrate a full range of widely used financial and operating performance measures. Five of them, American Optical, AT&T, Clorox, DuPont, and FMC, use some variation of economic value added. A sixth company, Meredith, is considering the adoption of an economic-value-added measure after completion of a company-wide, five-year program designed to achieve an ROE target. National Semiconductor uses a variant of the proprietary CFROI model. The Simon Property Group, an REIT, uses EBITDA and FFO. FFO is a measure unique to the real estate business.

The remaining case-study companies use a variety of cash-flow-based and earnings-based performance measures. Boeing replaced its accounting-based performance measures with a cash-flow-based measure that it believes is better correlated to the creation of shareholder value and also easier for its managers and employees to understand. The company's old financial metrics were profitability based on an ROE target and growth in annual sales. Its new metric is profitability and growth as measured by increased shareholder value over the long term. Boeing uses a valuation program based on a 20-year cash-flow projection in conjunction with traditional operating performance measures because it has very long product life cycles. The company routinely compares its internally calculated value with the actual market value of its stock. Each manager's objectives for a given year are part of an overall company plan to increase shareholder value.

PepsiCo emphasizes volume growth, operating profit growth, cash growth, and investment returns above the company's WACC as part of a balanced approach that includes a full range of financial performance measures. Federal Signal uses ROE, EPS growth, operating margins, and working capital measures as well as a DCF model to value the company, each of its business units, and potential acquisitions. Meredith uses ROE as its principal metric. Pioneer Hi-Bred uses ROE and growth in EPS at the corporate level and sets ROA targets at the business-unit level.

Table 2-2 lists the principal performance measures used by case-study companies.

TABLE 2-2 Principal Performance Measures Used by Case-Study Companies

Case-Study Company	Performance Measure
American Optical	Economic value added Return on net assets Free cash flow
AT&T	Economic value added Measured operating income Earnings-per-share growth
Boeing	Profitability and growth as measured by increased share holder value over the long term Traditional operating performance measures such as quality, cost, delivery, safety, and morale
Clorox	Economic value added
DuPont	After-tax operating income Cash flow Shareholder value added (a variant of economic value added) Return on net assets
Federal Signal	Sales growth Earnings-per-share growth Return on equity (corporate level) Return on net assets (business-unit level) Operating margins Working capital measures
FMC	Economic value added Balanced scorecard of financial and nonfinancial performance measures for each division
Meredith	Return on common equity
National Semiconductor	Cash flow return on investment (proprietary model)
PepsiCo	Volume growth Operating profit growth Cash growth Investment returns above cost of capital
Pioneer Hi-Bred	Earnings-per-share growth Return on equity (corporate level) Return on net assets (business-unit level)
Simon	Funds from operations Earnings before interest, depreciation, income taxes, and amortization Funds available for distribution

Mail Survey Respondents

Traditional financial performance measures continue to be widely used. Operating earnings was the measure most frequently cited in responses to the mail survey, followed by ROE, RONA, and TSR. A substantial number of companies continue to use ROA and ROI.

Twenty-six percent of those responding to the mail survey are now using economic value added as a metric and 21 percent are using CFROI. CFROI has different meanings. Two mail survey respondents use a proprietary CFROI model that is described in the National Semiconductor case study. Five mail survey respondents use the term in different ways:

☐ A chemical company associates CFROI with NPV analysis in capital budgeting.

☐ A mineral company defines CFROI as operating cash flow after working capital changes measured against the investment; the investment is defined basically as total assets minus current liabilities.

☐ An oil and gas company defines CFROI as the DCF rate of return from its capital investments.

☐ A computer manufacturer compares cash flow from operations to the level of assets employed for each business unit, evaluating every item on the statement of cash flows, or "sources and uses of funds" under "cash flows from operating activities" and "cash flows from investing activities."

☐ A high-technology company calculates pretax CFROI for each division. Free cash flow, defined as pretax income plus depreciation minus capital expenditures, is divided by the investment in each division, which is calculated as total assets minus current liabilities. No debt is included in current liabilities because divisions do not have debt.

Table 2-3 shows the distribution of financial performance measures used among the survey respondents. Other financial performance measures mentioned by respondents are listed in Appendix A.

TABLE 2-3 Financial Performance Measures Used by Survey Respondents

Financial Performance Measures	Percentage of Total Respondents
Earnings-Based Measures	
Operating earnings	72.5
Return on common equity	34.6
Return on net assets	32.7
Return on investment	26.8
Economic value added	26.1
Return on assets	21.6
Cash-Flow-Based Measures	
Total shareholder return	29.4
Cash flow return on investment	20.9
Other Measures	
Market value added	8.5

Several mail survey respondents described the performance measures they use in telephone interviews. An oil company measures incremental value from one year to the next by calculating a **perpetuity** each year based on normalized cash flows. A large consumer goods company uses the operating income return on capital employed to measure its business units. It sets targets based on comparable measures of peer companies that make that information available.

A large software company with more than 50 development and sales subsidiaries compensates the managing director and the finance director of each subsidiary based on operating earnings (90 percent) and days sales outstanding (10 percent). Days sales outstanding is an important measure in this business because the way receivables are managed is essentially the way cash flow is managed. When salespeople are having trouble reaching their targets, they sometimes offer unusually generous terms—in some cases as long as 365 days. The company does not want to penalize them but believes they should not get their full bonuses for sales made at the expense of such generous credit terms.

A large Canadian bank's financial objective is to maximize long-term shareholder value by achieving consistently superior earnings growth and return on common shareholders' equity while maintaining an appropriate dividend yield. The bank's goal is to achieve consistently superior performance relative to its peer groups across the primary measures of financial performance and condition, thereby achieving top-tier return on common shareholders' investment over the long term. To assess its financial performance and condition, the bank constantly monitors 10 key financial measures that balance profitability and prudential concerns:

1. Shareholder value, measured by ROI and increase in stock price;

2. Profitability, measured by ROE;

3. Earnings growth, measured by fully diluted EPS growth;

4. Revenue growth;

5. Productivity, measured by an overhead, or expense-to-revenue ratio;

6. Asset quality, measured by provision for credit losses as a percentage of average loans and acceptances;

7. Asset quality, measured by gross nonperforming loans as a percentage of equity and the allowance for credit losses;

8. Capital adequacy, measured by the Tier 1 regulatory ratio;

9. Liquidity, measured by the ratio of cash and securities to total assets; and

10. Credit rating, measured by the agency rating on the bank's public debt.

Other Measurement-Related Issues

Continued Use of Traditional Measures

Newer performance measures such as economic value added and CFROI usually supplement, rather than replace, more traditional accounting-based performance measures. AT&T and DuPont continue to measure their managers' performance based on conventional measures of earnings such as after-tax operating income (ATOI). DuPont continues to look at cash flow and its various components such as cash from operations at the business-unit level, net cash flow after capital expenditures, permanent investment turnover (sales divided by permanent investment), working capital turnover, variable margins, and fixed cost productivity (sales divided by controllable fixed costs).

Replacement of Unsuitable Metrics

Two case-study companies have found certain metrics unsuitable to their needs. Boeing finds that, because of the long-term nature of its development and production programs, together with its accounting conventions, accounting-based measures such as ROE are not good indicators of shareholder value creation. Economic value added would be difficult for Boeing to apply because of the long order and production cycle of the aerospace industry, the difficulty of making required accounting adjustments, and the difficulty of applying the cost of capital to an adjusted investment amount in this industry. National Semiconductor found that RONA did not give the signals that were required to continue reinvesting in its fast-growing industry.

More Attention to the Balance Sheet

An important objective of most value-based measures is to draw managers' attention to the balance sheet and efficient use of assets. Therefore, working-capital-turnover ratios (indicating the number of days accounts payable, accounts receivable, and inventory) still are considered important.

Separation of Investment Decisions from Financing Decisions

RONA, economic value added, and CFROI are measures of operating performance. As such, they are intended to be free from the influence of financing decisions. They should encourage managers to concentrate on achieving the highest returns from investments in their businesses without consideration of the methods of financing or financial structures of their business entities. RONA, as used by DuPont, is a measure of return on net assets; it is not influenced by the ratio between debt and equity. Economic value added, as used by American Optical, measures performance before interest cost and without consideration of capital structure. One of the reasons AT&T placed economic value added on its list of metrics is that existing measures such as ROE and EPS were potentially influenced by financing considerations. CFROI, used by National Semiconductor, is an internal-rate-of-return measure of current performance, also not influenced by the company's methods of financing. In a simplified measure of CFROI, rental expense is added back to operating income, and capitalized operating rental expenses are added to net assets. A similar adjustment is made by some users of the economic-value-added metric. When this is done, leasing is recognized as a financing decision that should not be of concern to operating managers. Without proper guidance, managers can view leasing as a way of improving returns without putting additional assets on the books.

Use of Both Operating and Nonfinancial Performance Measures

Case-study companies and mail survey respondents use a variety of operating performance and nonfinancial performance measures along with their financial metrics. These measures often are considered to be the value drivers that underlie financial performance and the creation of shareholder value. For example, Federal Signal has used measures such as operating margins and inventory turns for decades. Strategic objectives cascade into a valuation model and operating parameters to guide people in sales, manufacturing, and other functions throughout the company. Managers have revenue-growth, operating-margin, and working-capital-management objectives. Each component of inventory is managed carefully. "Finished goods" is an issue relating to service to the customer. "Work in progress" relates to the manufacturing cycle. "Raw materials" has to do with purchasing at the best prices, making sure suppliers stick to delivery schedules, and perhaps partnering with suppliers.

To improve cash flow, Boeing reminds its line managers to continue focusing on operating objectives with which they are already familiar: quality, cost, delivery, safety, and morale. Although line managers are gradually learning how their activities contribute to shareholder value, their primary job is still to focus on reducing defects and unit costs and improving cycle time, productivity, employee satisfaction, customer satisfaction, and market share. The company conducts frequent surveys to measure customer and employee satisfaction. These nonfinancial goals are consistent with the new value-based metrics because achieving them helps the company generate returns above its cost of capital.

Adaptation of Measures to Each Business

A number of case-study companies such as American Optical, Federal Signal, FMC, and Meredith are in several different businesses. In these companies, corporate management works with line business managers to develop appropriate operating measures for each business unit. FMC's businesses are measured with a balanced scorecard of financial and nonfinancial measures. Measures that drive each of the company's 25 businesses are developed in a bottom-up process. For example, the scorecards for agricultural chemicals and food machinery are very different. The balanced scorecard has focused senior management's attention on a number of nonfinancial measures that previously had little visibility. Those measures include market share; patents; new ideas implemented; new products moving from the development to the commercial stage; sales of new products; cycle times; customer complaints; late deliveries; amount of time to answer customer inquiries; and other measures of quality, innovativeness, and customer satisfaction.

3

How Companies Select and Implement Performance Measures

In deciding which performance measures to use, companies are concerned with how accurately these measures correlate with shareholder value and how difficult they are to implement with line managers. Companies have to evaluate the trade-off between accuracy and complexity.

In selecting new financial performance metrics, AT&T had four principal concerns: (1) representing shareholders' interests in price appreciation and dividends, (2) eliminating accounting biases, (3) incorporating all components of the planning process from long-term strategic planning to quarterly plan actual reviews, and (4) creating incentives for the right economic behavior. The company found that TSR was correlated best with long-term cash flows and to a lesser extent with economic value added. AT&T believes that economic value added offers the best compromise between accuracy and ease of implementation.

National Semiconductor chose the proprietary CFROI model with the belief that it predicts shareholder value more accurately than any other model and that it gives managers the signals they need to grow the business as well as increase returns. The semiconductor business is capital intensive and fast growing. It requires a company like National Semiconductor to continue investing or fall behind. The CFROI model helps the company justify investing in new plant and equipment, partly through adjusting all assets to current values. The RONA measure it used previously showed relatively high returns on depreciated assets and tended to discourage investment in new plant and equipment, which at current prices would reflect low returns. Like a number of other companies in the survey, National Semiconductor is aware that value is created by total dollars generated above the cost of capital, not by percentage returns alone. In adopting CFROI, National Semiconductor was aware that it would be complicated to explain to line managers. Managers of the company's eight divisions and their four- or five-person management teams use the model for strategic planning and investment choices, but managers below that level focus mainly on more traditional operating performance measures.

Clorox chose the economic-value-added metric even though it appeared that the CFROI model had a higher correlation with TSR. AT&T and FMC believe that earnings-based measures are easier for line business managers to understand than cash-flow-based measures. They believe that the economic-value-added measure is sufficient to motivate the right kind of behavior, for example, increased attention to working-capital management and fixed-asset investment.

Boeing, in contrast with AT&T and FMC, believes that its managers and employees can understand cash flow more easily than earnings. In the aircraft industry, quarterly earnings are not a good predictor of share value. Boeing had ROE and sales growth targets until recently. Those targets were difficult for managers to understand because they were based on accounting earnings, which are determined in large part by the program method of accounting for aircraft production. Boeing's managers are more comfortable with a model that ties traditional operating performance measures to longer term cash-flow projections that determine shareholder value.

Meredith and Pioneer Hi-Bred use a relatively simple measure, ROE, because they believe it is easy for people throughout the company to understand, and it drives the right kind of economic behavior. In 1992, Meredith set a five-year target for improvement in ROE and kept people focused on that goal until it was achieved. The company is now considering adopting economic value added. Pioneer Hi-Bred's principal financial performance measures are ROE and growth in EPS. The ROE concept has been a good tool for helping employees understand how the company makes financial decisions and sets financial goals. Managers are evaluated using two factors: the business unit's level of contribution compared to its target and the level of assets that are used. Pioneer uses ROA as a proxy for ROI at the business-unit level. In effect, it calculates RONA for its business units. Pioneer Hi-Bred does not currently feel a need for more complex financial measures to give managers the message to grow the top line as well as the bottom line. Meredith, Federal Signal, and PepsiCo are generally more concerned with a business unit's improvement over time using consistent measures than they are with the particular measures used.

Decision Making

Effect on Management

Financial performance measures ranging from ROE to CFROI have made line managers more cognizant of the balance sheet and asset utilization. At Clorox, for example, an economic-value-added metric has improved management of inventory, accounts receivable, and capital expenditures.

Clorox agrees with the philosophy incorporated in the economic-value-added metric that total capital invested should capture all amounts invested in a business from its inception. This includes money lost on disposed assets and failed business ventures, which management believes should be part of the total investment amount on which managers are responsible for earning a return, not just written off and forgotten.

Two case-study companies that have considered using economic value added, Federal Signal and PepsiCo, believe that this metric can discourage investment for growth if not used properly. This might occur if managers find eliminating assets in order to reduce capital charges to be easier than increasing earnings.

Delegation of Decision-Making and Spending Authority

The majority of case-study companies have adopted value-based performance metrics in conjunction with delegating increased decision-making authority and responsibility for generating cash flow and earnings to business units. The use of value-based performance metrics has tended to push all but the very largest capital budgeting decisions to the business-unit level. Business-unit managers often have authority for capital spending that fits within business plans and financial performance targets negotiated with corporate management. For example, at FMC, a capital expenditure as high as $2 million is presented to top management for approval because a decision of that magnitude often calls for an overall review of the business unit's performance and plans.

One of the most important changes at AT&T since the 1984 divestiture has been Chairman Robert Allen's initiative to reorganize the company into SBUs capable of competing in the market as if they were independent entities. Increased delegation of authority to business units and the development of economic-value-added business-unit performance measures resulted from that initiative[1].

The Role of the Finance Function in Performance Measurement

In several of the case-study companies, including American Optical, Clorox, Federal Signal, FMC, and Pioneer Hi-Bred, performance measures are developed jointly by line management and the finance function and approved by senior management. For example, at American Optical, performance measures and targets are recommended at the division level and are negotiated and approved at the corporate level. By participating actively in the development of their operating and financial performance measures, business-unit managers buy into the company's performance appraisal and compensation process.

At FMC, the control function has an important role in working with business-unit managers to develop financial performance measures, making sure they are understood and that they represent the results of each operation fairly and accurately. The controller's role at FMC goes far beyond financial measurement. Business-unit controllers are helping line managers make strategic decisions and understand the financial results of those decisions. They participate in the entire planning process, helping with pricing and sourcing decisions and other trade-offs to improve performance.

At DuPont, the finance function takes the lead in developing financial performance measures used throughout the corporation and in helping managers develop additional measures appropriate to their businesses. Each SBU has a financial manager who is in effect the CFO and part of the business leadership team. Financial managers from all the SBUs also work together as the company's finance leadership group, which has been involved in implementing DuPont's SVA measurement system and a project to create more accurate business-unit balance sheets.

---

[1]AT&T was interviewed shortly before its recent break-up was announced in September 1995.

At Pioneer Hi-Bred, the finance group plays an important role in the development of a balanced scorecard of financial and nonfinancial measures. It develops ideas, does analyses, makes recommendations, and works in partnership with business managers to determine whether certain measures can be effective in the management of a business. Finance helps business managers set their own benchmarks.

Effect of Measurement Systems on Financial Structure/Strategy

No company in the survey has changed its long-term financial strategy and structure based on the adoption of value-based performance measures. Boeing, Meredith, and Pioneer Hi-Bred believe that low leverage gives them the financial fortitude to weather economic cycles and base their planning on long-term creation of shareholder value. PepsiCo finds that a reasonable amount of leverage lowers its WACC and helps it grow, but the company would not borrow at a level that would jeopardize its investment-grade credit rating. Maintaining consistent financial structures helps these companies use consistent financial performance measures from year to year.

Internal Financial Reporting Systems

No performance measurement system can be effective if it is not supported by an accurate, timely information system. AT&T enhanced its internal information systems just as its new economic-value-added measures were being implemented. DuPont has a financial database that people from all SBUs can use for analysis and planning. Simon provides a comprehensive monthly report of operating results and performance measures to each of its shopping mall managers.

Explaining Performance Measures

For most companies, explaining the logic of value-based performance measures to nonfinancial people is a challenge. Clorox has used a board game based upon an imaginary company to make the process more understandable and enjoyable. Because the proprietary CFROI model is complex, National Semiconductor has explained it only to a limited number of senior managers.

Evaluation and Compensation of Management

Respondents to the mail survey report than an average of 41 percent of employees have compensation tied in some way to financial performance measures. The responses range from 1 to 100 percent. The median is 15 percent. For a quarter of the respondents, less than 5 percent of employees have compensation partly tied to financial performance measures, and for 22 percent of the respondents, 100 percent of the staff has compensation tied in some way to financial performance. It would appear that companies that answered 5 percent or less are referring primarily to incentive compensation programs for senior executives, and companies that answered 100 percent are referring primarily to profit-sharing programs that apply to all employees.

All of the case-study companies relate performance evaluation and compensation plans for senior management to the creation of shareholder value. At Clorox and Federal Signal, business-unit managers' bonuses are based mainly on business-unit performance, but partly on corporate performance as well. At American Optical, corporate management works with the management of each business to set targets and design bonus formulas based on a scenario of possible outcomes. Performance measures and targets are recommended at the division level and negotiated and approved at the corporate level. Five percent of a manager's base salary is awarded for successful completion of defined personal objectives.

At American Optical and Federal Signal, business-unit managers design performance metrics for managers reporting to them. For direct reports, compensation is partly based on value creation at the division level. For other managers, performance measures are more related to individual responsibilities.

American Optical and FMC have three-year plans based on economic value added for business-unit manager compensation. These plans are meant to encourage managers to set long-term performance targets. American Optical has two components in its compensation formula for division managers: economic value added for the year and the change in economic value added from the previous year. A manager's bonus each year has both a current and a deferred portion. At FMC, managers estimate economic value added for their businesses for the next three years, and the compensation system is based on those estimates. Pioneer Hi-Bred is considering a longer-term incentive plan driven by the increase in share value over a five- to ten-year period.

Management discretion plays a strong role in compensation at FMC and Federal Signal. At FMC, management evaluates each division's three-year plan for its degree of stretch. Plans with more ambitious earnings targets are assigned higher multipliers for potential bonuses. At Federal Signal, compensation for division presidents is in three components: salary, cash bonus, and a combination of stock awards and options. The CEO makes the decisions. Among his criteria are how well division presidents have carried out their strategic plans, how the performance of their businesses has improved over the last several years, how difficult their business plans have been to achieve, and how well they have attended to key **value drivers** such as sales growth.

Management discretion plays less of a role at Meredith and the Simon Property Group. Both companies remark that bonuses today are based more on hard numbers and less on discretion and the achievement of nonfinancial objectives than they used to be.

Several case-study companies have developed matrixes for bonus awards. In 1995, Federal Signal began to use a matrix for certain operating groups that defines a bonus level for each combination of sales growth and operating margin. Based on plans submitted, FMC's management develops a chart for each division indicating the level of earnings that qualifies for a bonus multiplier of zero, one, two, and three. The slope of the line is intended to encourage stretch targets. National Semiconductor has a performance award plan for executives based on ROE and a cumulative annual revenue growth rate (CAGR) that is used as a proxy for asset growth. A matrix compares ROE on the x-axis and CAGR on the y-axis. TSR equivalency lines, called "ISO-TSR" lines, are drawn on the matrix representing levels of TSR and corresponding levels of executive bonuses. Simon uses a matrix to determine incentive compensation for vice presidents of management, leasing, and development in each region. The matrix determines the percentage of each person's bonus that is determined by measures such as FFO, percentage occupancy, minimum rent, and specialty leasing income.

The case-study companies also have stock option and profit sharing programs. Each year, all Pioneer Hi-Bred employees share directly in the success of the company through a profit-sharing program. PepsiCo has a stock option program for all employees and an additional incentive-based stock option plan for senior- and middle-level managers. At

Boeing, executives on incentive compensation and selected non-executive level managers also receive stock options. Fifty-two managers of Simon, including all vice presidents and above, participate in a restricted stock incentive plan that is based on FFO performance over a five-year period with vesting occurring over nine years.

A large utility interviewed by telephone has an incentive plan covering all employees in which the total amount of bonuses is based on the company's ROE, and departmental and individual bonus levels are based on defined performance goals. The company has defined hundreds of performance measures tailored to individual jobs. A person's incentive measure may be based on a job-related measure such as customer satisfaction, but the amount of the person's bonus is also affected by the company's ROE.

A computer manufacturer has variable compensation for 80 percent of its employees now and a goal of 100 percent in the near future. Two hundred people in senior management have compensation based on a combination of corporate and individual performance. Managers in business units have compensation tied to a combination of business unit and personal performance. The level of corporate performance defines the size of the total bonus pot; individual performance defines a person's share of the pot.

For an oil company, a group of executives and managers comprising 20 percent of the staff receives performance bonuses based on corporate and individual performance. Bonuses range from 5 to 20 percent of a person's base salary, depending on seniority and influence. When the company was performing poorly in the early 1990s, bonuses were zero.

At a bank holding company, 85 percent of the workforce has some performance-related compensation. Employees throughout the company have the ability to earn between 5 and 15 percent of their base salaries in bonuses depending on their business units' performance in relation to plan. For managers, potential bonus compensation ranges from 15 to 75 percent of salary; more senior managers have higher percentages. The bank also has a restricted stock plan. An individual is awarded a certain number of shares but receives portions of the total award if and when the bank's stock reaches defined levels.

Conflict Between Short- and Long-term Measures

Some projects that reflect high NPVs or IRR based on DCF analysis may reduce a business unit's economic value added in earlier years because of higher capital charges for less depreciated assets acquired at current costs. In companies such as AT&T, DuPont, and FMC, business units tend to be large enough that projects in their early stages with low economic value added are balanced with other projects at more advanced stages with higher economic value added. Clorox continues using NPV analysis rather than the company's economic-profit-based CVM as a decision-making tool. Management is aware that even the most successful acquisitions and other large investments can depress the CVM for the first year or two. Sometimes managers have to be confident and patient enough to make decisions in one year that will benefit their CVM several years later—assuming they remain in their current assignments long enough to realize the rewards. American Optical provides managers with an incentive for performance improvement over the long run with bonuses that have both current and deferred portions. This also helps the actual level of bonus paid during down cycles. AT&T's managers are aware that there can be a conflict between the economic-value-added measure and monthly operating income, which ties directly into reported quarterly EPS and still is considered to be the most important performance measure for its managers.

Calculation of Amount of Capital Invested in Businesses

Capital invested in a business can be calculated based on either side of the balance sheet, historical capital invested (assets) or book stockholder equity plus debt, and about a quarter of the respondents to the mail survey do it each way. AT&T has equivalent definitions of capital on both sides of the balance sheet for economic-value-added purposes: (1) total assets (except cash) less non-interest-bearing liabilities and (2) equity, deferred taxes, and all long- and short-term debt, less cash. A dozen respondents to the mail survey indicated that they calculate capital invested in a business as net assets, or total assets minus non-interest-bearing current liabilities. One respondent uses the approximate current value of assets employed less operating liabilities.

A large regional bank holding company measures the performance of its subsidiary banks based on historical capital invested. The company expects that it will face more complicated capital allocation issues and start calculating risk-adjusted capital as traditional borrowing and lending become a smaller part of its business and trust and underwriting activities become more important. It will become less concerned with allocating historical capital invested and more concerned with how much risk each business entails and how much return it expects in relation to the amount of capital it is allocating. The holding company's senior vice president and treasurer says this is no different from pricing a loan.

Another bank holding company imputes capital to its businesses based on risk levels and industry norms. It is studying the use of imputed capital for an economic-value-added measurement system. A senior vice president believes that economic value added can be used for performance measurement in a bank holding company just as it can in any other business. The WACC at the holding company level is calculated just as it is with a nonfinancial company. Capital includes equity and subordinated debt, but not short-term debt. Based on comparison with similar companies, the holding company imputes a *beta* and a level of capital to each business that may be different from its book capital. For example, the trust business may be compared with banks specializing in trust, the credit card business with financial institutions specializing in credit cards.

For analysis purposes, the bank is also considering capitalizing start-up losses for new business, such as medical payments and origination costs for home equity, credit card, and other types of loans. For example, the bank may capitalize $5 million that it spends for a targeted mailing of one million pieces that is expected to produce 50,000 new credit card accounts. Over 18 to 24 months, the number of charge-offs, the revolving credit balances, and the overall return on the $5 million capital expenditure can be compared to the results of similar solicitations and used as a basis for measuring the performance of managers responsible for growing the business.

For a large food company, future-focused DCF is the primary measure; hence, invested capital is only a point of reference. The company evaluates returns on invested capital (fixed assets and operating working capital) compared to its cost of capital when it is considering whether to manufacture products in its own plants or outsource the production to another company.

An oil company calculates intrinsic values of business units for internal performance measurement based on the NPV of future cash flows. It determines "reasonable" capital structures for its business units based on those intrinsic values.

A bank holding company assigns capital based on various forms of risk, including credit, interest rate, operational, business, and disruption risk. An insurance company calculates required capital based on the riskiness of each product line.

Adjustments to Earnings and Capital Invested

Forty percent of the respondents to the mail survey make some adjustments to equity, and one quarter of the respondents make corresponding adjustments to NOPAT for performance measurement purposes. Among the most frequent adjustments are the capitalization of operating leases, adding **LIFO** (last-in, first-out) **reserves** to equity, adding deferred tax reserves to equity, and adding back cumulative goodwill amortization. The percentage of the group that makes various adjustments is summarized in Table 3-1. (Other adjustments to total capital invested mentioned by respondents are included in Appendix A.)

TABLE 3-1 Adjustments to Capital Invested

	Percentage of Companies that Make Adjustments	*Percentage of Total Respondents*
Capitalized operating leases	47.6	19.6
LIFO reserves	25.4	10.5
Deferred taxes	25.4	10.5
Cumulative goodwill amortization	23.8	9.8
Addition of unrecorded goodwill	20.6	8.5
Accrued postretirement benefit cost	20.6	8.5
Current value of property, plant, and equipment	15.9	6.5
Bad debt reserves	12.7	5.2
Warranty reserves/liability	6.3	2.6

Two-thirds of the companies that make adjustments to capital invested report they make corresponding adjustments to their earnings metrics.

The purpose of these adjustments is to gross up the accounting book value of equity and earnings to produce a more accurate economic book value and return. For example, some companies believe they can provide a truer measure of operating performance by capitalizing their operating leases. In so doing, they are recognizing lease-or-buy as purely a financing decision.

To save taxes, companies often use LIFO inventory accounting when prices are rising. With LIFO rather than FIFO (first-in, first-out) accounting, the cost of goods sold reflects the highest, most recent prices. Therefore, LIFO accounting results in a higher cost of goods sold and lower earnings for tax purposes than FIFO does. As a company continues to use LIFO, its inventory account becomes increasingly understated, and the difference between LIFO and FIFO accounting is accumulated in a LIFO reserve. Some companies believe that adjusting the inventory account back from LIFO to FIFO and adding the LIFO reserve back to the equity account can provide a better measure of replacement cost and capital, and adding the increase in the LIFO reserve back to earnings can reflect a company's unrealized gain from holding inventory that appreciates in value.

Some companies add deferred tax reserves back to equity and add back the increase in deferred tax reserves for a given year to NOPAT because they believe that deferred taxes will not be paid as long as the company continues to replenish the assets to which those deferrals are related (assets where depreciation is more accelerated for tax purposes than for book purposes). Making this adjustment to account for taxes not actually paid in cash is said to produce a truer cash-on-cash measure of business performance.

When one company buys another, it frequently pays more than book value. In this case, as much of the premium over book value as possible is allocated to specific assets, and the remainder is classified as goodwill. An acquiror's willingness to pay a given price for a company is often based on a DCF analysis just as any other capital investment decision is. Therefore, the accounting requirement to amortize goodwill and reflect that amortization in earnings is sometimes considered unrealistic and may discourage acquisitions that make economic sense. As a result, many users of economic value added and similar metrics adjust both their balance sheets and income statements to eliminate the effects of goodwill amortization. Similarly, they make adjustments for the "unrecorded goodwill" that arises when companies merge using pooling-of-interest accounting. With a pooling of interests, balance sheets are combined and adjustments are made in the equity accounts. As a result, the effective acquiror often acquires assets with unrealistically low book values. Adjusting for unrecorded goodwill brings those assets closer to current value and creates a more accurate measure of capital employed in the business and economic profit.

The case-study companies that use economic value added generally prefer to keep adjustments to capital invested as simple as possible and consistent with GAAP reporting. For FMC, capital employed for a business is primarily working capital, excluding bank and term debt, net property, plant and equipment, other operating investments, and goodwill. FMC's vice president and treasurer believes that if one of FMC's business units buys a company, it has to earn a return on the purchase price, and goodwill should be included in capital invested for performance measurement purposes. With the philosophy of accounting for every dollar invested, Clorox starts with its published balance sheet and adds back accumulated goodwill amortization, write-downs related to businesses it has restructured or sold, and adjusts investments in affiliates and minority interests to reflect actual investment levels. The CFO of a high-technology company that uses economic value added believes that the most effective tool is one that everyone can understand. He says, "If there are a whole lot of adjustments that only the accountants can understand, then the system is ineffective as a management tool."

The CFO of a business forms and equipment company says,

> We exclude non-interest-bearing current liabilities and equity in minority interests from our measure of capital invested. We used to make some adjustments such as capitalizing operating leases and adjusting property, plant, and equipment for current value. However, we stopped making those adjustments because the administrative cost was not worth the benefit, and we had difficulty with current-cost subjectivity.

Capitalized Research and Development Expenses

For a growing number of companies in today's knowledge- and technology-based economy, the intangible value of R&D is a more important asset than "hard" assets that are capitalized and found on the balance sheet. Under Financial Accounting Standards Board (FASB) Statement 2, almost all R&D expenses must be recognized when incurred. The only exception is development expenses for software products that will be sold. FASB Statement 86 permits those expenses to be capitalized after the company has ascertained that development of the product is technically feasible.

Few companies responding to the mail survey capitalize intangibles such as R&D and training for internal purposes when accounting rules do not allow them to capitalize those expenses on their financial statements. Only 2.6 percent capitalize R&D, only 1.9 percent capitalize training, and only 2.6 percent capitalize other intangible expenses that cannot be capitalized for accounting purposes.

R&D is the foundation for Pioneer Hi-Bred's current products and its future. The company does not capitalize R&D expenses, but treats them as though they were a capital asset in the strategic planning process. Moreover, the company believes that capitalizing R&D expenses would not change economic behavior, and it would require subjective decisions on amortizing those expenses and allocating them to business units. Pioneer Hi-Bred balances the amount it spends on R&D each year with its return-on-equity and EPS growth goals. Because of its long-term nature, R&D cannot be increased one year and decreased back the next. If additional funds were allocated, there would be a limit on how much could be absorbed. If R&D spending were cut back, some ongoing programs probably would be damaged.

A large pharmaceutical company that recently adopted economic value added is a notable exception. The company treasurer explains, "We have long development times for end products, and the payoff for those products is the engine that drives the business." Along with a number of economic-value-added advocates, he believes that writing off the $1 billion that the company spends on R&D each year is an accounting distortion because it suggests that the company "consumes" or realizes the benefit of those expenses in a 12-month period. As part of its economic-value-added measurement system, the company capitalizes $1 billion per year in R&D expenses and amortizes that amount over about eight years. Performance under the economic-value-added system is reviewed quarterly in conjunction with the company's plan/ actual review cycle. The treasurer notes that the accuracy of economic-value-added measurements has its limits. The company is trying to find the right balance between "administrivia" and using metrics that will tell it whether it is doing the right things to create shareholder wealth.

The treasurer of a large software company does not think his industry has addressed the issue of capitalizing R&D expenses very well. He observes that a decision to develop a product is typically made by one or more people fairly high in an organization. Based on such a decision, a company often hires developers and incurs other expenses without figuring out the total capital investment the new product will require. This treasurer thinks the problem with not capitalizing these development expenses is that people can too easily just forget about them. Often no one analyzes after the fact whether the product was a good idea or the company made any money on it. He thinks that companies could realize important marketing benefits by internally capitalizing every development dollar spent and analyzing the results of those expenditures.

According to this treasurer, a huge variation exists within the software industry in capitalizing R&D expenses, both internally and externally. His company is at the lower end of the spectrum, having capitalized $100 million in R&D and letting that amount remain constant for the past several years. In a few cases, R&D expenses have been capitalized in offshore subsidiaries where R&D and sales take place in the same subsidiary so that the unit will not be penalized in comparison with pure sales subsidiaries that have no such expenses. That is becoming less of a problem now because the R&D and sales functions in this company are now mostly located in separate subsidiaries.

The treasurer thinks it is ironic that bankers subtract the relatively small amount of capitalized R&D in their calculation of his company's tangible net worth when R&D is the single most important activity represented on the company's balance sheet. The company currently has a market capitalization of $20 billion and tangible net assets of just over $1 billion. The treasurer comments,

> Somehow $19 billion is missing. It is mostly tied-up, capitalized R&D and intellectual property rights. I have never won the argument with the rating agencies or the banks, but I fundamentally believe that they are wrong. It is the most valuable and the most tangible thing on the balance sheet. Something is tangible if people will pay for it.

The controller of a research-driven biopharmaceutical company explains that his company does not capitalize R&D because often the probability that a product will materialize is 1 in 10 or even 1 in 30. These expenses are very different from the kinds of development expenses related to the sale of software products that can be capitalized under FASB Statement 86, where there is a high degree of certainty that the asset can be used, and the company can estimate a useful life over which the expense can be amortized. The company has never considered capitalizing R&D expenses for the purpose of internal performance metrics. It has, however, capitalized R&D, sales and marketing, and even the value of brand names when using an intangible property overseas and determining the transfer price for tax purposes.

A dialysis machinery maker considers the amount of R&D expenses in the planning process each year. Only a small amount of its research is generic; most is product-focused. The company tries to layer its projects so that they will be in different stages of development at any point in time. If the project is successful, the company restates and capitalizes some prior expenses under the rules of project accounting. In doing this, it would prefer to err on the conservative side. The company has considered capitalizing R&D expenses internally, but believes there is too much potential for disagreement among different profit centers on how those expenses should be amortized and allocated.

4

How Shareholder Value
Is Created

In designing a value-based performance measurement system, a company must understand the objectives of the various types of investors who hold its stock and the methods those investors use to value its stock.

Investors' Objectives

Companies interviewed generally divide the population of investors between **momentum investors**, looking for short-term price movements, and long-term investors. Many observe that "sell-side" securities analysts still base their valuation mainly on EPS and price/earnings ratios. But many also believe that long-term investors who act as **lead steers** really try to estimate future cash flows and discount them at an appropriate rate such as a company's WACC.

AT&T and PepsiCo believe that quarterly earnings have a strong effect on the prices of their shares and have to be managed along with other measures such as economic value added or long-term cash flow. PepsiCo believes that a disappointing quarter could cause investors and analysts to question its long-term projections. Boeing, on the other hand, is in an industry where quarterly earnings are not a good indicator of shareholder value.

Boeing's vice president of Investor Relations believes that long-term investors, which include many of the largest pension funds and insurance companies, represent more capital than the momentum investors, even though the latter sometimes get more press. Boeing has made a conscious effort to make the dynamics of its business understandable to long-term investors, which it considers most appropriate for its stock.

FMC's vice president and treasurer also believes that the brightest investors are mostly concerned with the basic long-term cash-flow economics, but notes that this is hard for anyone to prove. She thinks that most valuation models are difficult to correlate with share prices. The controller of a biotechnology company finds stock prices in his industry to be volatile even though most institutional investors who hold the company's stock focus on the long term. In the biotechnology industry, there is little choice but to focus on long-term prospects because current earnings are relatively small in comparison. Analysts who cover this industry are supposedly long-term oriented, but they behave like momentum investors, frequently changing their underlying assumptions based on good news or bad news.

Valuation Methods

The central concept of value-based measures for the companies surveyed is achieving returns consistently above the cost of capital. Widespread agreement exists among the companies interviewed, as well as in the sources cited in the bibliography, that company valuations are based on expected future cash flows discounted at the company's WACC. However, methods for estimating future cash flows vary considerably.

The chief financial officer of a large food company tries to provide information to analysts and investors that will help them do their own DCF valuations. He says,

> Over time, the lead steers, the long-term investors who really make the market, focus on the right thing—the business and cash flows. They assign probabilities to them. They decide whether or not they are comfortable with a company's management and whether they believe management's projections. They do discounted cash flow valuations, and that is what sets the market. Whether or not EPS meet expectations has more to do with short-term trading.

Boeing, Federal Signal, and PepsiCo have internal models they use for calculating their own values and comparing them to current market values of their stocks. Boeing's model is based on a 20-year forecast. Federal Signal projects cash flows annually going out five years, and then calculates a 3 or 4 percent **growing perpetuity**. The director of

Corporate Development uses the model for the company as a whole, for divisions, and for potential acquisitions. He compares his internal corporate valuation with the current market price and a valuation done with a consensus of analysts' estimates.

Meredith is in two industries valued in different ways. Magazine publishers are valued based on revenues and earnings as well as cash flow. Broadcast businesses are measured primarily on cash flow. Consequently, some analysts value those businesses separately and compute a break-up value.

PepsiCo projects cash flows based on current strategies for each of its businesses. It values each business and then values the enterprise as a whole, comparing that value with PepsiCo's current market value. The strategic planning staff calculates valuations based on known strategies. Strategies include required investment and projected cash flow from new products, expansion plans, and capital required to sustain current operations. If a substantial difference exists between the internal valuation and the market's valuation, the staff tries to understand the reason. The market may not have enough information, it may not fully understand the company strategy, or it may simply be valuing the company strategy differently.

In projecting future cash flows, PepsiCo uses the **duration** of the company's long-term planning horizon, the point at which returns are not expected to exceed the cost of capital. The duration is currently 12 years. Planning is most detailed for the first three years. Although the 12-year forecast is far more detailed than a trend line, projected returns tend to move toward the cost of capital during that period. PepsiCo calculates durations used by comparable companies by doing a DCF valuation for each company based on (1) its growth rates and operating ratios, as forecasted by investment information service; (2) its WACC; and (3) its current market value, and then solving for duration as the unknown.

For REITs, DCF is not the preferred analytical method for either corporate valuation or investment decision making. Simon compares itself to its peers based on multiples of stock price to FFO. FFO is defined as net income from operating activities before the impact of depreciation and amortization of assets that are defined as unique to real estate. It is not the same as cash flow. Rental income, for the purpose of calculating FFO, is based on the average rate paid by a tenant for the entire lease, whereas in cash terms a tenant usually pays a base amount that steps up during the lease and sometimes enjoys a rent-free period at the beginning of the lease.

Correlation of Performance Measures to Shareholder Value

The methods used by investors and analysts to value a company, along with the key value drivers, are the foundation for establishing value-based performance measures. While it was rethinking its financial performance metrics, Boeing looked at correlation charts showing how well several different measures explained the share prices of publicly traded companies. It found a very low correlation between price/earnings ratios and EPS growth rates and only a slightly better correlation between the ratio of equity price to book value and ROE minus the cost of capital (calculated by the CAPM). There was a strong correlation between market price per share and predicted value per share based on analysts' published cash-flow forecasts. Boeing gathered evidence of the correlation of stock prices and long-term free cash flow prices from several sources. From this research, it was concluded that stock prices for Boeing and most other companies do indeed track cash-flow projections over longer periods, although there may be substantial volatility over shorter periods.

The proprietary CFROI model is believed by many to have a very accurate correlation with shareholder value, but as mentioned above, it also is considered to be complex to explain throughout the company and to use as a performance measurement tool. FMC found the CFROI model a helpful valuation and planning tool in the early 1980s as it was rationalizing its businesses and becoming a more focused conglomerate. Later, FMC found economic value added to be a better performance measurement tool because it was easier to explain to managers and more consistent with the earnings and book value of capital invested as published in the company's financial statements. At National Semiconductor, the CFROI model helps managers forecast the effects of their investment decisions on the value and TSR of their business units. It also encourages managers to make capital investments to grow with the industry and to improve their efficiency. It avoids the "old plant–new plant" trap in which RONA measures rise as equipment depreciates, creating a disincentive for new investment.

FMC's vice president and treasurer believes that the correlation of any model with the behavior of stock prices is difficult to prove empirically. Over the years, she has tried to predict FMC's share prices with several models but has not seen convincing results. She observes that people's conclusions about correlations are sometimes driven by their assumptions.

How Financial Risk Management Relates to Valuation

Some managers who believe that the values of their companies are determined by future free cash flow are concerned with the effect of foreign currency fluctuations on future cash flows. Accordingly, they may hedge foreign-currency-denominated cash flows two or even three years in the future. How far out they go is often determined by the cost of longer-dated options. However, no company interviewed for this study hedges long-term, future, foreign-currency-denominated cash flows with the stated objective of protecting shareholder value.

5

How Capital Budgeting Decisions Are Related to Performance Management

Performance metrics such as CFROI and economic value added are compatible with commonly used capital budgeting calculations such as NPV, IRR, and payback. There should be a logical connection between a company's capital budgeting methodology, the way it decides to invest in various projects, and the subsequent evaluation of business-unit performance.

Although it is possible to use discounted economic value added rather than DCFs for both capital budgeting and performance measurement, the case-study companies that use economic value added for performance measurement continue to use DCF analysis for capital budgeting. Because of its simplicity, calculating the payback for a proposed project is still popular in conjunction with NPV analysis.

All of the case-study companies except Simon use DCF analysis in some way for capital budgeting. Federal Signal requires different minimum IRRs for high-risk and low-risk projects.

All of the case-study companies that use economic value added as a performance measure use NPV analysis for long-term investment decision making. None of these companies has a problem reconciling the two. Generally, the companies that use economic value added believe that such an accrual-based system is well adapted to the evaluation of performance for any given year, and that cash-flow-based evaluation is more effective over a longer term.

While economic value added is used for planning, budgeting, and performance measurement at AT&T, traditional DCF analysis is still used for project evaluation and decision making. There has been some discussion that discounted economic value added is equal to DCF, and that therefore discounted economic value added could be used for decision making as well. However, several conditions, including required accounting adjustments and the timing of cash flows, must be met to ensure equality. Because of these conditions, AT&T believes that a model based on discounted economic value added would not be as flexible and would require more inputs than a model based on DCF.

American Optical is in the business of buying low-technology manufacturing companies and improving their operations. It does NPV and IRR calculations but places more emphasis on the estimated payback. The company likes to see projects with a two-year estimated payback but recognizes that actual project timing often slips behind schedule. A four-year payback roughly equates with the company's 25 percent cost of capital.

Most investment decisions for Simon are evaluated on a cash-on-cash basis. The only time the company uses NPV is in determining an up-front payment for a tenant who is breaking a lease.

An oil and gas company interviewed by telephone forecasts cash flows for a producing property for as many years as it can with a reasonable degree of assurance and then calculates a perpetuity and discounts it to the present. For example, it may be able to forecast cash flows for 5 years for a producing field with a 20-year estimated life. The WACC is used to discount cash flows for the first five years. It then calculates a perpetuity using a higher discount rate to reflect the depletion of reserves in the field.

Virtually all companies interviewed agree that capital budgeting decisions cannot be based on projected financial returns alone. Boeing encourages a balance between quantitative analysis and subjective judgment. Many companies are faced with more proposals than they can approve because of either capital or management constraints. A forest products company has an informal method of discussing "what-if" scenarios as it prioritizes projects that exceed its minimum return criteria or have lower returns but are necessary to maintain quality or protect assets. The company decides on a level of spending that is sufficient to maintain growth but is not so large as to strain financial or management capacity. Then it considers proposed projects in relation to each other. Management asks questions such as, What happens if we approve project A but not project B? What if we approve project A now and project B next time? Which projects could be spread out in time to give the company more flexibility?

Procedure for Submitting Proposals

For Boeing, FMC, and DuPont, capital budgeting proposals that fall within approved business plans for the year are approved at the division or business-unit level; only very large proposals are approved at the corporate level. DuPont's guidelines for a capital budgeting proposal require a description of the project and its rationale, alternatives to the project, economics and key uncertainties, and the effect of the project on a business unit's future financial performance. Quantitative analysis in a proposal includes a range of NPV outcomes, a range of **profitability index** outcomes and the NPV sensitivity to uncertainties for key variables such as product selling prices, market share, raw material prices, project cost, and market growth.

Financial and Nonfinancial Considerations

Nonfinancial considerations are well integrated into the capital budgeting process in all the case-study companies. For large decisions, DuPont frequently employs a method called decision and risk analysis to consider alternative strategies, analyze uncertainties, make decisions, and rigorously develop implementation plans. A multifunctional product team consults subject-matter experts and develops influence diagrams showing how key marketing, manufacturing, and technical uncertainties relate to each other and how they influence the projected NPV of the project.

Cost of Capital and Hurdle Rates

When asked how they determine their discount rates for capital budgeting, often known as hurdle rates, 35 percent of the mail survey respondents replied that they use the WACC or a hurdle rate related to the WACC. Another 6 percent mentioned the CAPM. In subsequent interviews, three of the companies that mentioned CAPM confirmed that they use this method for calculating the cost of equity and then calculate a WACC.

A number of companies interviewed recalculate their WACC annually. DuPont, on the other hand, believes that frequent fine-tuning is not a high priority for the finance function.

PepsiCo calculates a cost of capital for each business unit based on industry-derived *betas*. AT&T recalculates its WACC every year. The treasury staff develops a cost of equity based on a comparison with similar companies selected by a statistical procedure known as cluster analysis. This screening process chooses a group of companies similar to AT&T based on four variables: debt rating, interest coverage, asset turnover, and variability in operating income. AT&T then uses the average *beta* for this group of comparable companies to estimate its own cost-of-equity capital.

All of the companies interviewed, except Simon, use discount rates related to the WACC for capital budgeting analysis. Simon uses NPV analysis only when negotiating the up-front payment and other terms under which a tenant may break a lease. Some companies use the actual WACC and some have hurdle rates above the WACC.

Clorox, FMC, and National Semiconductor use real rather than nominal costs of capital. Clorox uses an 8 percent cost of capital assuming no inflation. Revenues and costs are projected using constant dollars. The company finds it easier to focus on volume increases, cost reductions, and operating margins when inflationary cost and price increases are not factored in. The CFROI methodology used by National Semiconductor incorporates a similar philosophy. CFROI is a real measure, net of inflation, that is compared to a real cost of capital. Constant dollar accounting is considered better than current or replacement cost accounting for asset values because it avoids the subjective element of determining replacement costs and focuses on the measurement of investments and returns in the same units of purchasing power.

A high-technology company uses a hurdle rate equal to its 20 percent target ROE for evaluating investments and acquisitions. The target return is based on its performance over the past several years and what it believes the market expects. The company believes that investments that do not meet this hurdle rate would dilute its performance. The hurdle rate for an engineering and construction company is an ROE target based on benchmarking with other publicly traded companies in similar businesses.

A large software company calculates a modified CAPM rate based on relative costs of borrowing in each country when it is acquiring distributors overseas. Because R&D is expensed, most of the company's capital budgeting is for leasehold improvements and office equipment. The company uses the cost of borrowing as a discount rate when it is deciding whether to pay up front for carpeting and other leasehold improvements or to have the landlord build those expenses into the lease.

Other methods mail survey respondents use for calculating the discount rate used in capital budgeting are listed in Appendix A. Among these methods are the following:

☐ country- or region-specific cost of capital

☐ long-term borrowing rate

☐ target ROE (bank)

☐ risk adjusted for equivalent stage of project (biotechnology company)

☐ benchmark ROI for corporation against competing companies

☐ ROI with *beta* for oil companies.

About half of the mail survey respondents use uniform discount rates throughout the business and about half use different discount rates for different business activities or investment opportunities. Two case-study companies, PepsiCo and AT&T, use higher discount rates for higher-risk projects. For example, PepsiCo uses 14 percent for most projects in the United States and Western Europe, but plans to use 18 percent for a prospective project in China. Federal Signal requires different minimum internal rates of return for approval of high- and low-risk projects. At FMC, people have talked about using different costs of capital for different businesses, but they have not found a way to gauge associated risks and determine effective costs for each business that would average out for the corporation as a whole. FMC's controller thinks that even if different rates were used for different businesses, the rates all would be within 1 or 2 percent of each other. The company prefers consistency and simplicity.

An oil company uses its overall WACC for all projects except for financing, for example, credit cards or receivables loans to distributors, where it uses a lower rate. A regional airline uses different discount rates for different asset lives. For some short-lived assets such as mainframe computers, where there is almost no residual value and the tax benefits cannot be used, the airline finds such a compelling case for leasing that it does not consider an NPV, lease-or-buy analysis necessary.

A biotechnology company uses higher hurdle rates for R&D projects at earlier stages when there is greater uncertainty, and lower hurdle rates at later stages. A high-technology manufacturer divides projects into risk profiles and assigns discount rates accordingly: 0 percent for safety and infrastructure projects, 15 percent for maintenance and cost reduction projects related to existing product lines, 20 percent for projects related to expansion of existing product lines, and 30 percent for new ventures and strategic investments.

A telephone company develops its discount rates based on a combination of business risk and financial risk. Business risk is based on earnings uncertainty and timing, size, complexity, strategic fit, and conformance to standards. Financial risk is based on capital structure, interest coverage, and expected cost.

Intangibles in Capital Budgeting Analysis

Although companies that responded to the mail survey generally do not capitalize research, development, and training expenses except for the few that are short term and product specific, these intangible expenses still are considered important in capital budgeting analysis. Thirty-seven percent of the survey respondents said their capital budgeting analysis includes investment for intangibles such as training, research, and development.

A large part of Pioneer Hi-Bred's value is based on intellectual property. The company's ability to develop new products and remain competitive is based on continued R&D. Budgeting for R&D is an integral part of Pioneer Hi-Bred's business planning. Yet the company does not capitalize R&D expenses for internal analysis, and NPV analysis plays only a small role in its research spending decisions. In deciding on research priorities, the company considers a whole portfolio of opportunities and uses matrices to compare expected rewards with factors such as the amount of investment required, the company's technological competitive position, the probability of technical success, and the estimated time required to bring a product to the market.

A mining company interviewed by telephone includes training expenses for installing a new computer system or for developing a new mine in its NPV capital budgeting analysis for those projects even though those expenses are not capitalized for accounting purposes. A forest products company capitalizes software development and training expenses related to the installation of new paper machines for performance measurement purposes and amortizes those expenses over a three- to five-year period.

Asset or Real Options

Twenty-one percent of the mail survey respondents indicated that they use **asset options**, also known as **real options**. Asset options are sometimes confused with financial options. Asset, or real, options include options to expand, contract, or defer projects and investments in future opportunities that may or may not materialize. For example, an investment in R&D or in a feasibility study might lead to another decision a year from now to either abandon the project or to make an additional investment. **Decision trees** may be used in this type of capital budgeting analysis. Other examples include the following:

☐ A company. may buy an option to open, close, or defer development of an open-pit coal mine.

☐ An owner of a lease on an undeveloped oil reserve may buy the right to acquire a developed reserve so that it will have the option to wait and invest in oil production until prices rise.

☐ A company may invest to build excess production capacity, in effect buying the option to invest further to actually increase production if market conditions are favorable.

☐ A company may invest more in a production process to design it in such a way that it has the ability to contract output in the future.

☐ A company may invest in a production process that can produce either of two products, thereby holding a switching option.

☐ A pharmaceutical company may invest in a project that has abandonment options at several different stages, for example, after initial R&D, after preclinical testing, after a first laboratory test, and after a second laboratory test.

Each of these examples, when analyzed with a decision tree and expected values, may have a higher NPV with the option taken into account than without it. (Decision trees are discussed in the next section.)

A Canadian oil company bids for leases that give it the right to explore land owned by provincial governments. On the leases it wins, it is obligated to spend a certain amount of money over a certain period of time. The amounts the company bids for leases and spends on exploration and development are all subject to NPV capital budgeting methodology. The controller of the oil company notes that some competitors take out financial derivatives and sell their production forward, locking in their prices for up to 10 years and retaining only operating risk.

Decision Trees and Probability Analysis

Forty percent of the respondents to the mail survey indicate that their capital budgeting analysis includes decision trees, **multiple possible outcomes**, or some other form of probability analysis. Boeing, DuPont, and Pioneer Hi-Bred generally find that calculating a **range of possible outcomes** is a more effective way to account for project risks than the adjustment of discount rates, using higher discount rates for higher risk. At DuPont, key uncertainties for a project are identified and a range of possible outcomes is quantified for each uncertainty over the range of 10 to 90 percent probability. For example, a business may believe that there is a 10 percent chance of selling 10 million units or more, a 50 percent chance of selling eight million units or more, or a 90 percent chance of selling seven million units or more. An analysis of NPV sensitivity to uncertainties is done based on 10, 50, and 90 percent probabilities for variables such as project cost, raw material prices, product selling prices, market share, and market growth. The effect that each variable could have on the project is quantified assuming all other variables are held at the 50 percent probability level.

A high-technology company interviewed by telephone projects cash flows related to a piece of capital equipment and then does a what-if analysis. Sales may be 20 percent less than expected next year; profit may be less than expected. Realistic scenarios are quantified in NPV terms.

A utility uses an informal system of probability analysis in the procurement of generating capacity. The company's objective is to run its various nuclear and coal plants at lowest cost and to minimize the likelihood of being unable to service load requirements at a particular time. Nuclear plants have high fixed costs and low operating costs, and coal plants have low fixed costs but high operating costs. The company does a probability analysis of likely outcomes, tries to minimize the costs, but pays a little extra for the assurance of having sufficient generating capacity for estimated peak power requirements.

An oil company uses probability distributions to calculate expected values of cash flows in its DCF analysis, for example, assigning a 70 percent probability to one outcome and a 30 percent probability to an alternative outcome and adding the two for an expected value. It uses decision trees for some large projects such as refineries or offshore platforms that have several stages and for projects where not all decisions are made up front. Additional investment, go/no-go, and other decisions may be made at the second, third, or fourth stage of a project for various reasons, including market conditions and how well the previous stages have worked out.

A defense contractor quantifies the probability of "go" as whether or not a project will be funded, and the probability of "win" as whether or not the company will win the project if it is funded. For the planning process, the company multiplies the dollar value of the contracts by the composite probability of go/win, and for the largest contracts, it tries to predict whether it will win them or not. The company believes this is the best method to determine a "most likely" value in its intensely competitive and volatile market environment.

The CFO of a food company prefers to assign probabilities to estimated future cash flows than to raise the discount rate for increased risk. He believes that assigning probabilities requires a person to address business issues more specifically, and that raising the discount rate amounts to "making a broad generalization." When his company prepares a proposal for an overseas plant, it assigns probabilities to each year's cash flows based on an analysis of the competitive, economic, and political climate. It may think there is a 30 percent probability that problems in a given year will cause cash flows to be reduced by a certain amount, perhaps 40 percent, and a 5 percent probability that the project will be a total failure. It considers factors such as remittance risk, the risk that taxation will change, the partner's business reputation, the partner's experience in the food business, and possible disputes with the partner over dividend policy.

A pharmaceutical company uses **Monte Carlo simulations** and probability-adjusted outcomes in making go/no-go and priority decisions as it periodically reviews its portfolio of molecular compounds in the R&D pipeline. At each stage of a project, scientists estimate the probability of success of that project as it surmounts various technical hurdles. Marketing and manufacturing people assign probabilities to various other parts of the value-chain analysis.

6

American Optical Corporation

American Optical Corporation and its affiliated companies comprise a $200 million enterprise owned by a former McKinsey consultant and investment banker whose specialty is recognizing and buying undervalued low-technology businesses, improving their operating and financial performance, and selling at the right opportunity. The corporation's current businesses include ophthalmic lenses, specialty lens systems, bonded abrasives, and steel tubing.

The owner's distinct competence is in buying capital assets at bargain prices and improving the operating efficiency of the business. The company uses a variety of measures to track overall efficiency improvement, including macro measures such as revenues per employee and more specific measures such as contribution per minute for each mill (in the case of the tubing business).

Criteria for Buying Businesses

American Optical generally looks for underperforming businesses, frequently those that no longer fit the strategy of large corporations. The core of the lens business was purchased under such circumstances, after having suffered severe losses under previous ownership. American Optical may expand an existing line of business by buying companies, operating units, or capital assets from other companies in the same industry. For example, it expanded its lens business by acquiring leading optical companies in the United Kingdom and Brazil. Sometimes American Optical can even add value to businesses in contracting markets. For instance, the amount of grinding in manufacturing operations has declined in recent years because of manufacturing process improvements. American Optical has bought a number of marginal grinding wheel companies, improved their efficiency, consolidated their operations, and removed excess capacity. As a result, it has grown tenfold in the past 20 years and become one of the leading companies in sales and profitability in the domestic abrasives industry.

Improving Business Performance

American Optical seeks to develop measures that quantify changes in operating performance and provide continuous feedback. For example, its tubing company measures mill efficiency by daily tracking sales dollars per minute and contribution per minute for each shift. Other important measures include sales dollars per hundred feet produced, overhead per hundred feet produced, and net capital asset cost per million feet produced.

Financial Performance Measures

Performance measures and targets are recommended at the division level and negotiated and approved at the corporate level. John van Dyke, CFO, requires a minimum of three measures for each division: economic value added, RONA, and free cash flow. Business-unit managers participate actively in the development of their operating and financial performance measures and thus buy into the company's performance appraisal and compensation process.

American Optical has defined a hurdle rate of 25 percent pretax RONA for its divisions. This rate represents the company's WACC. In calculating that average, the company assumes that the cost of equity is about 35 percent. Division managers have no role in the formulation of capital structure for their businesses, so their performance is measured before interest cost and without consideration of capital structure.

Net assets are essentially total assets less non-interest-bearing liabilities. Assets for the purpose of this calculation are essentially the same as reported in the company's financial statements. Accounting policies are adopted in a way that minimizes the difference between cash earnings and accounting earnings. The company prefers to avoid adjustments to keep the measurement system as simple and understandable as possible. RONA excludes financing considerations, so external debt is not deducted from net assets, and earnings are before interest charges. Economic value added is the pretax dollar return in excess of the 25 percent hurdle rate.

Although minimum performance standards expressed in terms of economic value added are common among all businesses, actual return targets may differ substantially. Corporate management works with the management of each business to set targets and design bonus formulas based on possible outcomes. The 25 percent hurdle rate sets a minimum standard of performance. If the division is not currently performing at that level, or even if it is losing money, the hurdle rate provides a corporate standard to aim for. In the case of an underperforming business, a manager is compensated for the change in the return on invested capital from year to year until the hurdle rate is achieved. The company believes in high rewards for bringing about change in underperforming businesses.

Van Dyke believes that the minimum return target and a standard measure such as economic value added for quantifying change offer an objective approach to performance evaluation. The approach makes managers' goals clear and consistent. It prevents managers from making excuses for poor performance or emphasizing other measures disproportionately. Bonuses are based on economic value added and the change in economic value added from year to year. This formula separates bonus compensation from budgets and eliminates budget negotiations between the business and corporate management. The budget becomes the tool a manager uses within the business to achieve an economic-value-added goal. Results become the objective, and how aggressive the budget is in relation to that objective depends more on the manager's style than on negotiations with corporate management. Van Dyke says, "It's up to the general manager to come up with projects and figure out how to increase the return. The budget then becomes the tool, and the bonus formula is the way he gets rewarded. The trick is to make these elements as parallel as possible."

Before deciding to use the economic-value-added measure, the company measured its ophthalmic division on management pretax profit, which provided for a capital charge of 12 percent. But 12 percent was not high enough to make managers pay real attention to the balance sheet. For example, the reward for increasing profits by $100 was eight times as high as the reward for reducing inventory by $100. Even with the 25 percent hurdle rate, where the ratio is four to one, managers sometimes pay too little attention to the balance sheet.

Incentive Compensation

American Optical has two components in its compensation formula for division managers: (1) economic value added for the year and (2) the change in economic value added from the previous year. The actual formula and the two components are weighted based on what corporate management thinks the objectives for the business should be. Van Dyke says, "You have to get in and understand the dynamics of the business and come up with a compensation formula that is specific to a business to reward its senior managers."

A manager's bonus has both a current and a deferred portion. This formula provides an incentive for sustained performance improvement and can *help* the level of actual bonus paid during down cycles. Van Dyke points out that the lack of any cap on bonuses lifts people's horizons. It opens their minds to the potential of their businesses. And as mentioned earlier, it eliminates negotiation over each year's budget. Also, five percent of the manager's base salary is awarded for successful completion of personal objectives. At the beginning of the year, the president of the company and the manager of an operating unit agree on a maximum of five personal objectives. Those objectives might include things that do not have immediate financial impact—for example, deciding on hardware and software and installing a new information system. General managers establish bonus programs for their direct reports, which mirror the concepts of their own compensation plans.

Table 6-1 shows an example of a projected bonus plan for a subsidiary in a cyclical business. A likely future scenario has been projected with sharp increases in performance targeted to take place in fiscal years 1995 and 1996, followed by a significant economic downturn in fiscal 1997 and two years of recovery to surpass the prerecession peak. For fiscal year 1995, the economic value added for the subsidiary is $3.6 million, representing an improvement of $1.1 million. Assume a typical general manager's salary is $100,000, with a target bonus of $25,000. The manager's bonus bank is established at the beginning of the initial year at twice the target bonus, or $50,000. The formula for the manager's bonus is 1 percent of economic value added, the earnings for the division after deducting a 25 percent capital charge on net assets, plus 3.5 percent of the change in economic value added from the prior year. Thus, the formula is strongly weighted toward improved earnings.

One percent of $3.6 million economic value added is $36,000, and 3.5 percent of the improvement in economic value added is $39,000. Those two bonus components plus the beginning bonus bank balance of $50,000 bring the total balance to $125,000. One-third of the bank balance—$41,000—is paid in the current year, leaving a balance of $84,000. Additionally, $5,000 may be paid each year based on the accomplishment of personal objectives. This example shows a significant increase in the annual bonus award, but the actual bonus paid is only a small fraction of the improved financial performance brought about by significant productivity improvements.

The subsidiary is in a cyclical business. A recession is predicted for 1997, which causes the subsidiary's economic value added to decline by $1.5 million for the year. The component of the bonus related to the level of economic value added at the end of 1997 is $46,000, and the component related to the change in economic value added is ($53,000), resulting in a net subtraction of $7,000 from the bonus bank. Because the balance in the bonus bank declines, the manager's one-third payout also declines. However, the manager's bonus is not affected as drastically as it would have been if it were based entirely on 1997 results. After 1997, the division's growth resumes, and the manager's bonus picks up as well. Thus, the bank extends the horizon of the manager beyond one year and makes him accountable for the future performance of the business.

TABLE 6-1 Sample Bonus Calculation *(in thousands)*

Fiscal Year	1995	1996	1997	1998	1999
Economic value added	$3,600	$6,100	$4,600	$5,600	$6,600
Beginning bank balance	50	84	156	100	128
Bonus components:					
Economic value added	36	61	46	56	66
Change in economic value added	39	88	(53)	35	35
Total	125	233	149	191	229
One-third payout	41	77	49	63	76
Ending bank balance	84	156	100	128	153
Personal objectives bonus	6	6	6	6	6

Bonus Formula: 1% of economic value added + 3.5% of change in economic value added

In the first year a manager is measured under this system, the company makes a loan to create a balance in the bonus bank. The bank vests in equal annual increments over a seven-year period. There are a number of special provisions for payout. When an employee retires, becomes disabled, or dies, the entire vested amount is paid out. When an employee leaves the company or is terminated without cause, two-thirds of the vested amount is paid out. When an employee is terminated with cause, there is no payout.

Other Operating Measures

American Optical uses other operating measures not directly related to the bonus plan as benchmarks for improving the performance of its manufacturing operations. One productivity guideline that has been particularly effective is revenues per employee. In 1986, revenues per employee in one division were $62,000. The CEO told the division manager that world-class manufacturing companies were then operating with revenues per employee in excess of $100,000. Consequently, the division manager was told to raise the productivity of his division to $100,000. The division manager initially disagreed with the CEO, but managers in other companies and some business school professors he talked to did not think such a target was out of line. So he asked the CEO to allow him three months to develop a plan. The resulting plan included required capital investment that would bring productivity revenues up to $100,000 per employee. When the business was sold four years later, revenues per employee had reached $106,000.

Approval of Capital Investments

American Optical has a standard capital investment request procedure for all divisions. The procedure is in the form of a computer disk that formats the financial analysis and draws attention to the information that must be entered. The program requires both working-capital items and fixed-investment items to be included in the overall investment decision. Internal rate of return, economic value added, and payback are automatically calculated by the program. Of the three calculations, priority is given to the payback with emphasis on paybacks of two years or less. This two-year target recognizes that investment requests tend to have very optimistic economic benefit forecasts and implementation timetables. Estimated two-year paybacks often become three- or four-year paybacks in reality. A four-year payback is roughly equal to the company's 25 percent cost of capital.

Identifying a comprehensive list of capital investments is an integral part of each division's budget process. Projects are ranked in terms of both payback and strategic importance. A capital expenditure figure is budgeted based on likely approvals and the anticipated timing of the expenditures. Often, projects are added or substituted during the year, and many of them do not get beyond the rigorous review process at the division level. Significant capital investment requests are signed off on by the division financial directors and general managers, sent to Al Skott, Vice President and Corporate Controller, and then finally approved by the CFO and the president.

People Interviewed

Allen I Skott, Vice President and Corporate Controller
John W. van Dyke, Senior Vice President and Chief Financial Officer

7

AT&T Corp.

AT&T uses the economic-value-added metric for its 20 strategic business units (SBUs) and most of its sub-units. Other sub-units that share assets or liabilities and do not have complete sets of financial statements use a modified version. The company adopted the new metric as part of an effort to make people think more competitively. Compensation for 110,000 AT&T management employees in the United States is tied to economic value added.

The company has two parallel measures it considers equally important, though perhaps more difficult to measure: (1) people value added, relating to associates and employees and (2) customer value added. For the finance function, customer value added is primarily a measure of how well business units within AT&T are being served.

Developing an Entrepreneurial Culture

One of the most important changes in AT&T since the 1984 divestiture has been Chairman Robert Allen's initiative to reorganize the company into SBUs.[1] After the breakup, AT&T was still largely regulated and had a regulatory mentality. People were insulated and not close to the markets. They were accustomed to thinking in terms of functions within the company rather than competition with the outside world. For example, in the old AT&T, a central department had done all the marketing for the 22 Bell companies. After the breakup, AT&T's businesses faced increased local

---

[1]The company was interviewed shortly before its September 1995 announcement of plans to break into three businesses.

competition, and MCI and Sprint challenged its long-distance franchise. To respond, managers had to be able to take more direct responsibility for customers, products, and markets. The balky line-of-business organization was not up to the task. AT&T needed smaller, leaner business units that could compete in the market as if they were independent entities.

Limitations of Existing Performance Measures

In the mid-1980s, the company adopted a financial measure for business units called "measured operating income." It was just an operating profit measure—revenues minus costs and expenses (plus other income). The measure offered one advantage: it was easy to apply across many diverse businesses. But it did not account for cash flow or attempt in any way to reflect balance sheets for business units.

In 1990, the finance function made a case that cash flow was important, and net operating cash flow became a new monthly measure for each business unit, reported to senior management and the board of directors. But managers were not held accountable for cash flow in their performance evaluations as they were for measured operating income. And despite its importance, cash flow had inherent weaknesses as a performance measure. The timing of cash flows is not always predictable; for example, they are affected by the amount of payables and receivables on the balance sheet at the end of the period. Annual cash flow is also affected by financing decisions. A manager can avoid the necessary cash outflow for a capital expenditure for a piece of equipment by deciding to lease the equipment.

When the finance function saw the thrust of Allen's redirection, it decided that the company's existing measures were inadequate. They did not capture the true profitability and financial performance of the business units. A team in the controller function led by Serge Wind, Assistant Controller—Financial Studies, began developing a new set of measures consistent with the company's new direction.

Criteria for New Performance Measures

The finance function had four principal concerns as it started to design new performance measures:

1. **Representing Shareholders' Interests.** Performance measures should represent shareholders' interests. Shareholders' financial interest in dividends and price appreciation best correlated over the long term, first with cash flows and second with economic value added. Studies showed that measures such as earnings per share, return on equity, and growth in net income correlated poorly with shareholder value.

2. **Eliminating Accounting Biases.** Existing measures such as ROE and EPS had built-in biases related to the accounting model. The amount of equity was affected by write-downs. The number of shares outstanding was affected by whether the company had recently issued more debt or more equity. These measures were potentially distorted by financing considerations. Because they were based on the income statement, they did not reflect important information found on the balance sheet and the cash-flow statement, such as business or financial (leverage) risk or resources being used.

3. **Transcending Components of the Planning Process.** A new measurement system would have to transcend all the components of the planning process. AT&T was designing a new comprehensive planning process beginning with long-term strategic considerations and moving to 5- and 10-year business plans, to resource allocation considerations, to budgeting for the following year, and finally to a plan-actual review of the budget year. The company wanted to be able to refer to the same metrics throughout the process. It would not be useful to talk about return on equity for the long term and then talk about earnings per share for the budget year.

4. **Creating Incentives for Economic Behavior.** The company wanted measures related to long- and short-term business performance that could be used to evaluate and compensate its management staff. The measurement system would have to be consistent from one year to the next and give management appropriate incentives for action.

Decision to Adopt Economic Value Added

If people were to be empowered to run competitive business units with delineated products and services, they would have to be responsible for all the resources those units needed. They would have to be accountable for the assets used. Managers would have to learn about balance sheets and cash flows. In some way, the new measurement system would have to take into account the creation of shareholder value based on the principles of net present value. This way of thinking was new. Wind recalls, "We didn't have to worry about financing before divestiture. Every five weeks or so, we just rolled out a huge bond issue. We were highly rated and there was no problem. At the time of divestiture, we had so much cash lying around we didn't know what to do with it."

So even though AT&T wanted managers to be aware of cash flow and to learn how to manage it, the company was still more comfortable with an earnings-based performance measure. Wind says, "People resonate more comfortably with earnings from the income statement." Economic value added is an earnings measure, but it also takes into account assets utilized and the cost of capital.

Cost of Capital and Hurdle Rates

AT&T uses a uniform cost of capital for its economic-value-added measurement except for its financial services units such as the Universal Card and AT&T Capital Corporation, which have higher debt ratios and therefore lower costs of capital. The weighted average cost of capital for the corporation is computed each year. The cost of equity is developed based on a comparison with similar companies that are selected by a statistical procedure known as cluster analysis. This screening process chooses a group of companies similar to AT&T based on four variables: debt rating, interest coverage, asset turnover, and variability in operating income. AT&T then uses the average *beta* for this group of comparable companies to estimate its own cost-of-equity capital.

A uniform cost of capital across all nonfinancial business units had the advantage of simplicity as the company was implementing a new measurement system. The CFO wanted business-unit managers to worry about their returns rather than differences of percentage points in their costs of capital. However, Greg Wilensky, Treasury Manager, says that now that the basic system is up and running, the finance function may reexamine the use of different costs of capital for business units based on inherent risk and comparison with other companies in similar businesses.

Wind points out that the company is competing not only to sell its products and services but also to attract investment capital. As business managers invest in various projects and attempt to create shareholder value, they have to think about investors who have many alternative ways to invest their capital. The economic-value-added measure helps managers explain to investors how well the unit is performing.

Treasury is responsible for advising business units on appropriate discount rates for capital budgeting analysis and decision making. Those rates are normally higher than the cost of capital used for economic-value-added performance measurement for some business units, and they are adjusted upward for higher-risk projects. The company's 12 percent WACC for 1995 is used for projects with normal business risk in the United States, as well as for global projects whose revenue is not dependent on a single economy. The cost of capital is routinely adjusted to compensate for projects with higher-than-normal business risk. The additional premium could be anywhere from 50 to 500 basis points depending on the nature of the project. In addition to project-specific risk, the company adds a country risk premium to projects that derive a significant portion of their revenue from a single economy. Country risk premiums have a wide range—from 30 basis points for a G7 country to more than 1,000 basis points for a country in an emerging market.

Once a project is accepted and implemented, it is evaluated with the rest of the business at the cost of capital. AT&T considers it neither practical nor useful to evaluate the performance of different projects within a business unit at different hurdle rates. Presumably, using higher hurdle rates for evaluation and approval increases the likelihood that projects will indeed earn more than the cost of capital.

Creating Balance Sheets for Business Units

AT&T has 20 strategic business units with distinctly defined products and services. Two of the best known examples are business communication services and consumer communication services, which provide long-distance service. Each SBU has a large number of sub-units.

To implement economic value added, a balance sheet was aligned with each SBU. Sub-units have economic-value-added measures as well, but some share too many assets for separate balance sheets to be practical. SBUs have agreed to adopt some assets and liabilities that might otherwise be considered corporate. The company has developed a chart of accounts for converting statements prepared according to GAAP to the economic-value-added measurement system.

The Economic-Value-Added Methodology Committee, headed by Wind, has defined how every account and subaccount on the balance sheet and income statement should be treated for calculation of economic value added. For the balance sheet alone, this calculation has required making decisions on more than 500 accounts. Some items have turned out to be more complicated than they seemed in the beginning. For example, interest income and expense appeared to be associated with financing, and therefore not part of the economic-value-added computation. Then the methodology committee came across a case of interest income from sales-type leases and interest income earned on advance payments for contracts, and decided that it had to add a new account called non-capital-related interest income to the economic-value-added measurement system. The account includes interest income deemed to be from operations and therefore not considered pure financing income.

Measurement of Economic Value Added

Economic value added is computed as after-tax earnings minus the cost of capital based on average capital for the period concerned. Philosophically, AT&T has tried to measure the aggregate sum of capital supplied by investors since the company was founded, and to measure return on that capital in a way that approximates a cash-on-cash return as closely as possible without requiring excessive accounting adjustments. The company has two equivalent definitions of capital for economic-value-added purposes, one based on the left-hand side of the balance sheet, and the other based on the right-hand side. On the left side, capital is essentially total assets (except cash) less non-interest-bearing liabilities. On the right side, capital is equity, deferred taxes, and all long- and short-term debt, less cash.

Relatively few adjustments are made to accounts on the left-hand side. Amortization of goodwill and certain other write-downs are reversed. Property, plant, and equipment are essentially at book value with no current value adjustment.

The methodology committee followed six principles in developing the metric, defining capital, and making adjustments for the SBUs: (1) motivate desired behavior, (2) keep it simple and accurate, (3) provide a fair and level playing field going forward, (4) facilitate a consistent methodology across all business units and across the financial services business units, (5) track operational and financial performance to enable clear accountability, and (6) enable the assessment of economic value added performance at the AT&T consolidation level by summing the economic value added performance of the various business units, divisions, and eliminations created in consolidation. The overarching principle is to motivate behavior that adds to shareholder value.

AT&T redesigned its entire internal management reporting system when economic value added was implemented. The system now translates monthly budget, actual, and variance figures, prepared according to GAAP, into monthly economic-value-added reports. Reports for top management that delineate drivers responsible for deviation in the economic-value-added measure, and even viewgraphs for presentations are prepared automatically.

Now that the economic-value-added system is in place and seasoned for product/service business units, the next challenge is to extend the metric to the company's international operations. Among the issues that the company will have to address are transfer pricing among U.S. and overseas units, translation of overseas subsidiary financial statements into the parent functional currency and then into the economic-value-added system, and treatment of hedging expenses. It is difficult to create balance sheets for some business units—sales subsidiaries, for example—if a "full-stream" perspective is desired to evaluate performance. A full-stream perspective for an overseas sales unit would reflect the cost of all assets utilized in manufacturing and preparing products for sale rather than treating the sales unit as just a retailer that bought the product and sold it at a margin.

Capital Budgeting

While economic value added is used for planning, budgeting, and performance measurement, traditional discounted cash-flow analysis is still used for project evaluation and decision making. There has been some discussion that discounted economic value added is equal to DCF, and that discounted economic value added could thus be used for decision making as well. However, several conditions, including required accounting adjustments and the timing of cash flows, must be met to ensure equality. Because of these conditions, a model based on discounted economic value added would not be as flexible and would require more inputs than a model based on DCF.

Tying Economic Value Added to Compensation

Wind believes that the chairman's support and the tie to individual compensation are the two factors that have most helped economic value added succeed as a performance measure at AT&T. About 110,000 of AT&T's 300,000 employees are considered management, with compensation affected by the economic-value-added measure. The new measures are designed to give people a broad indication of the types of economic behavior and financial results that the company thinks will build shareholder value. In using these objective measures, management has implicitly said that it cannot ride herd on every decision in a company so large, and that each business unit and, to a lesser degree, each individual has to take on the responsibility of building shareholder value.

How the New Metrics Have Changed Behavior

The new metrics have changed behavior within AT&T in a number of positive ways. Economic value added gives everyone a uniform, simple measure of what the company believes will enhance shareholder value. Because a business unit's economic value added is not affected by the method of financing, the measure has helped separate business and financing decisions. The importance of traditional operating measures such as accounts receivable turnover and inventory turnover has been underscored because managers can see the effect of those measures on economic value added.

As a caveat, Wind notes that not everyone clearly understands the distinction between a single-period measure, such as economic value added used for performance measurement, and multiperiod measures, such as NPV and IRR used for investment decisions. Some managers are still reticent about projects that have positive net present values but will depress economic value added in the first year or two. One solution to this problem is for managers to have faith in the positive effect on economic value added that the project will have several years in the future, but keeping such faith is difficult when managers are transferred to new assignments every two or three years. Wind also points out that even though managers make commitments in terms of economic value added, the metric does not mitigate the importance of a business unit's monthly and quarterly measured operating income. With a few adjustments related to taxes and interest, those monthly and quarterly business-unit results add up to the company's earnings per share. AT&T believes that quarterly earnings per share have a strong influence on its stock price.

Looking at the company's experience to date, Wind observes that the economic-value-added measurement system has been accepted more readily than he would have believed possible. Everyone is using it and talking about it as a link to managing the company's assets well and balancing customers' and shareholders' needs better. It is not just a formula or calculation, but a way of looking at things. In February 1995, the Economic-Value-Added Methodology Committee had a meeting with all the financial vice presidents to discuss a number of refinements in the measurement system. In those discussions, all participants supported continued use of the system.

People Interviewed

Paul Riley, Treasury Manager—Corporate Finance (AT&T)
Greg Wilensky, Treasury Manager—Corporate Finance (AT&T)
Serge Wind, Assistant Controller—Financial Studies (AT&T Network
    Systems)

8

The Boeing Company

Boeing recently introduced new financial metrics that will help with strategic planning and provide an element for incentive compensation. They are based on shareholder value as calculated by estimated long-term cash flows. The company believes that the new metrics will be more effective than its previous accounting-based metrics, which did not correlate well with the market price of its stock, were difficult to link with performance targets for operating groups, and did not directly recognize the cost of capital.

Boeing's defined mission is to be the number one aerospace company in the world and among the premier industrial concerns in terms of quality, profitability, and growth. Until recently, the company's fundamental goals were (1) quality as measured by customer, employee, and community satisfaction; (2) profitability as measured against its ability to achieve and maintain 20 percent average annual return on stockholders' equity; and (3) growth over the long term as measured against a goal to achieve greater than 5 percent average real sales growth. Now, Boeing has decided to replace its ROE and sales-growth metrics with a new metric—profitability and growth as measured by increased shareholder value over the long term.

Share Price Analysis

While it was rethinking its financial performance metrics, Boeing looked at correlation charts showing how well several different measures explained the share prices of publicly traded companies. There was a very low correlation between price/earnings ratios and EPS growth rates. There was a somewhat better correlation between the ratio of equity price to book value and ROE minus the cost of capital (calculated by the CAPM). There was a strong correlation between market price per share and predicted value per share based on analysts' published cash-flow forecasts.

Boeing gathered evidence of the correlation of stock prices and long-term free cash flow from several sources. This research was the basis for its conclusion that stock prices for Boeing and most other companies indeed do track cash-flow projections over long periods, though there may be substantial volatility over short periods. The research conclusions and the revised metric were supported by the efforts of Larry Bishop, Vice President—Investor Relations. Bishop embarked on a program to cultivate the segment of the investor population that has a long-term outlook and values companies based on DCF projections.

Boeing may be better able than many other companies to project revenues and expenses over the long term because of its market position and the long-term nature of its development, order-to-delivery, and customer support cycles. In the *Current Market Outlook,* published annually by Boeing's commercial airline group, world air travel demand and airplane supply requirements are forecast for the next 20 years. Although cash-flow projections over such a long horizon may appear speculative, the company makes multibillion dollar investment decisions based on its long-term forecasts. It believes that if the forecasts are good enough for such large investment decisions, they should be good enough for valuation and performance measures.

Problems with Accounting-Based Metrics

The ROE target that Boeing used in the past was focused on historical performance. It was based on accounting earnings, which are determined in large part by the program method of accounting for aircraft production. Boeing has used the program method to account for aircraft unit costs since the mid-1960s. Under this method, the unit cost is an average cost based on a conservative estimate of how many aircraft will be sold. The pattern of earnings is substantially different from the pattern of cash flows. When a new model is developed, a large negative cash flow for design and tooling occurs over several years. For the 777, more than $3 billion was spent on tooling and booked as inventory before the first plane was delivered. There is also a learning curve; unit costs generally decrease during the course of a program. On the military side of its business, Boeing uses contract accounting that is similar in concept and raises the same kinds of cash-versus-accrual issues as program accounting.

Economic Value Added Difficult to Apply

As it was rethinking its financial performance metrics, Boeing considered whether economic value added would be a meaningful measure. The company believes in the economic profit concept but decided that economic value added was not appropriate because of (1) the difficulty of making the required accounting adjustments and (2) the long order and production cycles of the industry.

Applying the cost of capital to an adjusted investment amount would not be easy with Boeing's accounting system. The company would have to determine which R&D expenses, if any, should be capitalized, and how they should be amortized. The number of years over which to amortize R&D would be a subjective decision because product life cycles are difficult to estimate. The first 747 was delivered in 1969, and deliveries are still forecasted for 15 years from now. A major program such as the 747 tends to spawn derivatives that benefit from the original development expense. Gary Beil, Vice President and Controller, says, "To implement a metric like economic value added, you would have to do some complicated accounting and try to simulate the economics to come up with this investment number, when in reality all that matters is cash flow. Why not just look at cash flow?"

Boeing's earnings are determined by total expected program costs and delivery and economic cycles. Accounting earnings for a given year are not a reliable measure of the company's economic performance. Looking back over the past 15 years, Boeing found that economic value added does not explain its own market value added as well as it might explain the values of companies in some other industries. In some peak earnings years such as 1992, Boeing's market value added declined because its stock price reflected a decrease in orders and future earnings expectations. Beil admits that economic value added might make sense for a company with a product life cycle of 5 years or less, but not for a company like Boeing with a 20-year horizon.

Shareholder Value Analysis Plan

Because accounting-based measures such as economic value added did not seem appropriate, and because Boeing can reasonably project revenues and costs for many years into the future, the company decided to calculate its own share value based on projected cash flows and to use that value as a basis for planning and performance evaluation. The company has recently implemented its Shareholder Value Analysis (SVA) plan to align incentive compensation for its top executives with its long-range, cash-flow-based plan to create increased shareholder value. It has begun a program to explain to all levels the importance of cash flow, cost of capital, and how financial and nonfinancial performance measures tie together as indicators of shareholder value.

Each year, the company prepares its long-range plan and a more detailed 2-year plan that is used for most performance commitments. It calculates market capitalization based on cash flows in the long-range plan discounted at its WACC. It periodically updates the discounted cash-flow value for major strategic decisions, new program commitments, major productivity investment decisions, market forecast changes, and performance. Executives are encouraged not to be overly optimistic and submit forecasts they cannot meet.

At the end of the year, the company compares its expected market value with the actual market value, taking changes in assumptions into account, and analyzes both internal and external factors that caused the difference. It assesses management performance based on the reasons it believes the company's share value has changed. If the stock price has risen only because of external economic factors, then management may not be rewarded for it. If management has implemented a program that is expected to generate cash flow in the future and the market has not yet recognized it, then management may have to wait for its reward until the market does recognize it.

The SVA process is designed to make the strategic planning and decision-making processes more rigorous, to reinforce the company's current operating performance measures, and to improve the analysis of both internal and external factors that affect the company's stock price. Boeing is trying to make managers at all levels aware of the importance of sound economic decision making. It explains SVA as a disciplined framework to help managers make decisions and identify options, not as a formula to blindly drive decision making.

Integrating Financial and Nonfinancial Measures

Boeing explains to all managers how the company's financial and nonfinancial goals are linked to the overall goal of increased shareholder value. Management believes that the primary drivers of increased shareholder value are good strategic, tactical, and operating decisions; constant improvements in processes that enhance cash flow; and external economic and political factors.

Boeing reminds its line managers that to improve cash flow and build shareholder value, they must continue focusing on operating objectives they are already familiar with: quality, cost, delivery, safety, and morale. While line managers are gradually learning how their activities contribute to shareholder value, their primary job is still to focus on reducing defects and unit costs and improving process cycle time, productivity, employee satisfaction, customer satisfaction, and market share. The company conducts frequent surveys to measure customer and employee satisfaction. These nonfinancial goals are consistent with the new value-based metrics because achieving them helps the company generate returns above its cost of capital and, directly or indirectly, affects cash flow.

Boeing also has other internal profit targets. For example, business-unit managers in the commercial airplane group are measured by operating profit contribution, which is not an accounting measure of earnings but an approximate gain per airplane unit. It is a measure of how well costs are moving down the projected learning curve.

Financial Education for Line Managers

Because the SVA plan was just introduced this year, most line managers have not yet learned the rationale behind the new financial metrics. The company has begun its education program to explain to all managers how the things they do are tied to cash flow and shareholder value. In training programs, Boeing is explaining the fundamentals of DCF, net present value, and corporate valuation. The firm emphasizes to managers that many of them are shareholders through a stock option plan, a 401(k) plan, or both, and that increasing shareholder value is consistent with customer, employee, and community satisfaction. Some companies have chosen economic-value-added measures because they are easy to explain and they relate to reported earnings, but Boeing believes that cash-flow measures are easier to explain to its line managers than accounting-based measures.

Incentive Compensation

Boeing has implemented a new incentive compensation program for its senior managers based partly on the creation of shareholder value. For the company's top executives, between 30 and 100 percent of incentive compensation is based on measures that include quality as determined by customer, employee, and community satisfaction, and whether the company has met the objectives of the long-range plan used for increasing shareholder value. A portion of the compensation is in the form of stock that vests in three years.

The company is using both relative and absolute performance to measure its performance against the goal of creating shareholder value. On a relative basis, the company compares itself to the S&P 500, the S&P Aerospace Index, and 20 premier benchmark companies. On an absolute basis, it measures increasing shareholder value based on its after-tax cost of capital.

For executives in the product groups, 30 percent of incentive compensation is based on the company performance discussed earlier and 70 percent is based on group and individual performance. The primary group performance measures are traditional operating measures such as profit contribution, unit cost, cycle time, and market share. Managers in the groups understand how these measures tie into cash flow and the creation of shareholder value.

Executives on incentive compensation also receive stock options, which gives them an additional reason to be concerned with how their own performance affects cash flow and how cash flow affects the value of the company. Both the stock, which vests in three years, and the options, which vest over five years, give managers an incentive to make decisions based on a long-term perspective.

In addition, in July 1996, Boeing announced the establishment of a $1 billion stock investment trust for an incentive program, called the ShareValue Program, that allows employees to share in the results of their efforts to increase shareholder value over the long term. The trust, called the Boeing ShareValue Trust, will hold only Boeing common stock.

Boeing President and CEO Phil Condit announced the ShareValue Program in a communication to all employees. In it, he said, "The ShareValue Program is intended to focus the attention of all Boeing people on what we can do—both as individuals and working together—to increase the return to people who invest their money in Boeing. If we do that, the people of Boeing will share directly in the success they help create."

Employees of The Boeing Company and its susidiaries are eligible to participate in the ShareValue Program if they do not already participate in the executive incentive plan. The program's investment is divided into two overlapping periods, with $500 million in each period (both began July 1, 1996). Period 1 runs two years, through June 1998; Period 2 runs for four years, through June 2000. All other investment periods will be four years in length and overlap an existing period.

Distributions will be in the form of Boeing stock. Employees could receive a distribution of stock following the end of each investment period, depending on how much the fund investment has grown. Distribution will be determined by the total dollar return (the increase or decrease in Boeing share price plus the reinvestment of dividends) achieved above a minimum level during an investment period. The program requires a return on investment or threshold rate of 3 percent per year, compounded annually on the fund's starting value, before distributions will be made. Distributions are possible every two years—in 1998, 2000, 2002, and so forth.

"Period 1 is only two years long because we didn't want employees to wait four years to have their first opportunity to receive a distribution," Condit noted. "The four-year investment periods reflect our emphasis on increasing shareholder value over the long term, consistent with the company's fundamental goal. At the same time, overlapping periods allow for more frequent potential distributions."

There would be no distribution if the return on the trust investment averages 3 percent or less per year at the end of an investment period. "While there is no guaranteed distribution, there is plenty of opportunity for us to do the right things to create value," said Condit.

The 3 percent per year threshold rate, compounded annually, is designed to allow the trust to retain some of its potential gains in order to grow the base level of the investment in Boeing stock. "This threshold is a mechanism that allows for building compounded growth into the stock investment, creating the possibility of greater distributions in future years," said Condit.

Capital Budgeting

Most of Boeing's capital spending decisions are made within its major operating groups—commercial aircraft and defense and space—as part of larger approved programs. In their investment proposals, managers are encouraged to provide a balance between quantitative analysis and more subjective judgment. The weighted after-tax average cost of capital is used as the discount rate for NPV analysis unless unusual risk factors that require a higher discount rate are involved.

When making strategic decisions such as going ahead with new aircraft models or derivatives, managers are encouraged to calculate multiple possible outcomes and to look at the total impact of various alternatives. For example, they might address what happens to sales of the 767 as a result of a derivative program to increase seating on the 757. The company prefers to take various project risks into account by calculating multiple outcomes rather than by adjusting the discount rate. Also, a consistent discount rate is easier to explain to managers than a discount rate that is adjusted subjectively based on a project's risk. People are encouraged to think carefully about both the midpoint and the range of expected possible outcomes. An estimate of just plus or minus 10 percent is not a satisfactory analysis. If the midpoint is too close to the most optimistic scenario, managers may be too optimistic; if it is too close to the bottom, they may be too pessimistic.

Appealing to Value Investors

In addition to understanding internal forecasts and how they affect the value of the company, Boeing's management believes that it is also important to understand the viewpoint of the investment community. Bishop believes that the majority of investment dollars in the market are from long-term investors such as pension funds and insurance companies, even though so-called momentum investors are sometimes more visible and influence the shorter-term movements of every company's stock. Bishop explains that different shareholders have different investment objectives and different criteria for valuing the company's stock. Mutual fund managers are often momentum investors. They have short horizons because of pressure to produce quarterly results. They are interested in cyclical patterns and other factors that will move a stock over a short period of time. When their objectives have been met or not met, they sell and move on. The higher the portion of momentum investors that hold a company's stock, the more volatile the stock price will be.

Sell-side security analysts often cater to the needs of momentum investors because those investors generate the highest volume of transactions. In contrast, buy-side analysts and money managers for insurance companies and corporate and public pension funds are more interested in preservation of capital and returns over the long run. Although they are partly judged on quarterly performance, they do not bail out just because a company fails to meet earnings expectations for a quarter or two. While momentum investors are more interested in current EPS and price-earnings ratios, value investors tend to be more interested in cash flow over the long term.

In the past, Boeing believed that it was being defined in the market by sell-side analysts. Boeing needed to approach the type of investors most appropriate for its stock and define itself. Bishop and his colleagues began working more actively with long-term investors and making sure they understood the company and its business and financial dynamics, particularly the long-term cash-flow projections that underlay its share value. By talking to value investors when the company was in the down part of its cycle and its stock price was a long-term bargain, Bishop and his colleagues were able to attract a substantial class of investors.

As a result of these efforts, the composition of Boeing's investors has changed substantially. Between December 1990 and June 1995, the number of Boeing's shares held by long-term value investors doubled while shares held by individual investors decreased. The shares held by growth or momentum investors fluctuated sharply with the company's earnings cycles; the shares held by index investors stayed about the same.

Financial Structure

Boeing's policy is to maintain a conservative financial structure with low leverage. Boyd Givan, Senior Vice President and Chief Financial Officer, believes that a maximum debt-to-equity ratio of about 30 percent optimizes the company's cost of capital and helps protect its investment-grade credit rating because of the deep cyclical nature of the airplane business. He believes that the company's underlying financial strength helps it take a long-term view, spanning across economic cycles. It also provides assurance to investors that the company has the ability to carry out its long-term strategic plan. Givan says, "I think we have now convinced S&P and Moody's that we can operate through a down cycle and still maintain our financial strength."

Forecasting capital needs is particularly challenging for Boeing because of business cycles and the huge cost of developing a new aircraft. Boeing could conceivably be increasing its dividend payout and buying back stock one year, only to raise long-term capital to fund an acquisition or a development program a few years later. Possible future programs such as very large capacity transports or second-generation supersonic planes, still only being discussed in the industry, might be too large even for a company like Boeing to undertake without a partner. Maintaining a conservative capital structure helps the company position itself for those and other future opportunities. It also helps provide the financial stability Boeing needs to carry out its long-term plan to enhance shareholder value.

People Interviewed

Gary W. Beil, Vice President and Controller
Larry A. Bishop, Vice President—Investor Relations
Paul S. Gifford, Director—Investor Relations
Boyd E. Givan, Senior Vice President and Chief Financial Officer
Jon J. Johnson, Manager—Boeing Commercial Airplane Group
    Accounting
David L. Sjogren, Assistant Controller, Corporate Accounting and
    Financial Analysis

9

The Clorox Company

The Clorox Company traces its beginnings to 1913 when it was established to produce liquid bleach. The business grew rapidly and was acquired by Procter & Gamble (P&G) in 1957. In 1969, a Supreme Court order forced P&G to divest Clorox, still a one-product business. While the company had a strong franchise and cash generator in the Clorox brand, management felt a strong need to diversify. It made some excellent acquisitions of grocery store products. It also acquired other product lines that did not fit the company's core competency in marketing consumer goods through grocery stores and, later, through large discount distribution channels. The company overinvested in manufacturing capacity; its ROA began to slip and its stock performed poorly. Clorox lacked a precise definition of where it wanted to go and what was needed to get there.

When Craig Sullivan became CEO in 1992, he set priorities that helped the company capitalize on its core strengths and sharpen its focus. He also began a comprehensive strategic review with senior management. Management determined that it would trim the company's portfolio to businesses that it understands and where it could use its competencies in R&D, manufacturing, and marketing to build brands and add consumer value. Clorox sold its restaurant equipment, bottled water, and frozen foods businesses. Its remaining businesses were organized into three large groups: household products (laundry and cleaning products), Kingsford products (charcoal, insecticides, and cat litter), and food products (dressings and sauces). Sullivan encouraged product managers to "fast-track" the product development process, making decisions with less data and more judgment—in other words, being less risk-averse. Two company-wide initiatives also were launched: The work simplification initiative addresses the need to eliminate work that does not add value. The customer interface redesign initiative is designed to enhance the value delivered to consumers by simplifying and improving the systems and processes that interface with trade customers. It focuses on product promotion; customer order entry and fulfillment; and billing and collection of payments.

Adoption of Clorox Value Measure

Management developed its Clorox Value Measure (CVM), a variant of economic value added, to focus people in all functions on what creates shareholder value. The measure helps managers identify trade-offs among growth, operating margin, and utilization of assets.

A group of senior financial managers evaluated several overall metrics the company might use, including conventional accounting measures such as return on assets and return on equity; growth measures such as sales and volume growth; and margins. They wanted a measure that would correlate with shareholder return, and they wanted an ongoing operating measure that related net present value analysis of new investments to the evaluation of ongoing operations. In their view, the two best choices were the proprietary CFROI model and economic value added. CFROI appeared to have a higher correlation with shareholder value but seemed more difficult to explain to most operating people. Management believed that a measure based on the economic-value-added concept would be easier to explain and implement. Lloyd Chasey, Director of Finance and Accounting for the Household Products Division, says, "I wouldn't feel as good about this if we had a theoretically purer model that didn't catch on."

CVM is defined as net operating profit after taxes (NOPAT) less a capital charge of 12 percent times average assets employed. Management's reasoning for implementing the measure is as follows:

- ☐ It has a higher correlation with TSR than traditional accounting measures.

- ☐ It places greater emphasis on balance sheet management along with a historical focus on the income statement.

- ☐ It is expected to be representative of performance in the long term even while major investments with positive net present values, such as acquisitions or heavy new product spending, may depress CVM goals in the short term.

☐ It is reasonably simple for operating managers to understand and act on.

☐ Strong CVM growth will lead to long-term EPS or ROE growth, or both.

CVM Calculation

As mentioned earlier, CVM is calculated as NOPAT less a capital charge for assets utilized. The calculation of NOPAT and average assets employed is shown in Table 9-1 below.

TABLE 9-1 Calculation of NOPAT and Average Assets Employed

Net Operating Profit After Taxes (NOPAT)

    Earnings Before Income Taxes

    Add back: Restructuring reserves

                    (Gain)/Loss on sale of assets

                    Intangible amortization

                    Interest expense

    Multiply the sum by one minus the corporate statutory tax rate.

    Add back: Tax shield on intangible amortization

Average Assets Employed

    Current Assets

    Subtract: Current liabilities (excluding commercial paper and current portion of long-term debt)

    Net Property, Plant, and Equipment

    Add back: Net intangible assets

                    Accumulated amortization

                    Other assets

                    Restructured assets

                    Investment in affiliates

                    Minority interest

                    Change in cumulative translation adjustment

The tax shield on intangible amortization is added back to earnings because a recent change in tax law enables the company to realize a tax benefit on its deduction for the amortization of goodwill over a 15-year period. Construction in progress is deducted from net property, plant, and equipment so as not to penalize managers for assets that are not yet producing returns. Management realizes that some oppose such a deduction because they believe that average assets employed should include every dollar invested. Accounting for every dollar invested is the philosophy behind adding back accumulated amortization to net intangible assets, adding back restructured assets such as write-downs of the company's investments related to the detergent and bottled water businesses, and adding back investments in affiliates and minority interests not reflected on the balance sheet.

Some companies that use economic value added capitalize research and development expenditures and make a number of other adjustments to capital and earnings. Some make adjustments that charge economic rather than book depreciation. Clorox prefers a simpler application and does not believe that the CVM would deliver a different message if it made all those adjustments.

Changes in Business Decision Making

CVM has led to a primary behavioral change—a heightened awareness of the balance sheet as well as the income statement. Clorox management traditionally has focused on market share, volume growth, and advertising and promotion budgets. Marketing, manufacturing, and other operating people always have understood profit margins, but until CVM was implemented, they did not really understand the balance sheet. Because Clorox always had strong cash flows, the cost of cash was not an issue for managers. CVM has made operating managers focus on cash and the balance sheet, which now have a real bearing on their compensation.

Brand managers in the past were not sufficiently aware of the cost of excess plant capacity and high inventories and receivables. The new metrics encourage them to make fewer proposals for additional plant capacity, to offer less extended terms to customers, to design less complex promotion programs, and to introduce fewer SKUs. SKU is an industry term for stock-keeping units, which are sizes, flavors, or other product variations. Increasing the number of SKUs raises production expenses and required levels of inventory, makes the overall business more complicated and time-consuming to run, and requires more management time.

With CVM, managers immediately saw that their capital charges would be lower if they spent less on plant and equipment. In 1994, Clorox's capital spending was $57 million (about 3 percent of sales) compared with $78 million in 1993 (5 percent of sales), and $156 million in 1992 (12 percent of sales). In the past, there were no penalties for investing in excess plant capacity; it was better to have too much than too little. No expense was too much to avoid being out of stock. Now there is more emphasis on fully utilizing available capacity and not putting extra money into "frills."

CVM has encouraged brand managers to simplify their promotion programs. In the past, complex programs increased production expense and working capital requirements in several ways. Plants had to produce extra inventory for shipment to stores during the promotion period. Sometimes a program called for plants to manufacture and ship complex pallets of merchandise—for example, six or eight varieties of Hidden Valley Ranch salad dressing in specific quantities. Preparing the pallets required extra work in the plant, and unsold stocks with expired purchase dates often were returned at the company's expense.

Promotion programs frequently provided discounts, and in many cases, customers paid less than invoice amounts, explaining that the invoices did not reflect the discounts. Salespeople often did not follow up to resolve the disputed items, and large amounts were written off.

Keith Tandowsky, Director of Finance and Accounting for the Kingsford Products Division, thinks that prior to CVM the company generally had done a good job of making new investment decisions and managing its profit margins, but had been less effective at reducing its asset base and discontinuing unprofitable operations. Now managers are more willing to discontinue products and divest assets. They know that their profits will be reduced but that their assets will be reduced to a greater degree, thereby improving their CVM.

Karen Rose, Vice President and Treasurer, likes to think of DCF as a decision-making tool and of CVM as more of a mindset. For example, CVM training has helped salespeople understand the impact of sales promotions and SKU proliferation. They once equated what they spent on the trade with the amount of volume they could expect. Now they understand the impact of this spending on inventory and trade credit as well.

Incentive Compensation

Part of compensation for vice presidents, directors in SBUs, and senior managers is tied to CVM. Approximately eight SBUs—each with a management team of four or five directors—are responsible for groups of brands. An SBU does not have an actual head; typically, its management team consists of a director of marketing, a director of manufacturing, a director of finance, a director of sales, and a technical center representative for research and development. Each manager is eligible for a bonus that is calculated on a target of about 25 percent of base salary. Typically, 50 percent of the bonus is based on the SBU's performance, 25 percent on corporate performance, and 25 percent on functional performance measures and other objectives that an individual and his or her boss have agreed to at the beginning of the year. The director of finance and accounting might have individual goals such as developing a cost-savings program, helping brand managers develop more accurate forecasts so a lower safety stock of plant inventory is required, or working with brand managers to reduce deductions from customer invoice payments.

Corporate staff members at the director level who are not in SBUs have a similar incentive program. Fifty percent of their bonuses is based on company performance and 50 percent on individual performance.

An SBU submits to senior management what the company calls a "firm forecast" of volume, cash flow, profit targets, and balance sheet items. It negotiates what is needed to meet the business unit's objectives and the company's growth and earnings objectives. Sometimes, management will ask that the targets be raised. Then SBU managers translate those objectives into specific goals for operating margin, asset turnover, and volume growth, which are put on a matrix and used as a basis for compensation.

SBU directors provide updated forecasts of profits, cash flow, and the balance sheet to the company's management committee about three times a year. Every month, they provide reports showing gross margin, operating margin, asset turnover, the component of inventory turnover, and days sales outstanding. They discuss the reasons for variances and their plans to meet established targets in the coming months.

Senior managers below the director level have a similar program with a maximum 150 percent payout. Senior managers include brand managers in the marketing organization, as well as managers of analysis and control and managers of cost on the finance side.

Below the senior manager level, each operation has its own traditional operating performance measures. Manufacturing units have measures such as cost per case, cases per labor hour, and other productivity and safety measures. The company has not extended CVM to the plant level, though it may do so at some time. Now it tells plant managers that if they are doing a good job controlling their capital spending, costs, and asset turnover, they are contributing to CVM. SBU managers visit the plants periodically to explain the link between what they are doing and CVM.

Implementation Issues

The CVM measure has been accepted well in the company, at least philosophically. A few issues of execution still remain to be worked out. For example, some directors do not think that CVM gives business units sufficient incentive to invest for the long term. A division may have to invest heavily in a given year to rejuvenate a brand or to acquire a business at a substantial premium. CVM will go down that year. Targets are developed year to year. Some think the program would encourage managers to take a longer-term view if it had a banking system for bonuses in which a manager gets paid only one-third of a year's bonus the year it is earned, and the other two-thirds of the bonus are deferred. Under such a system, a manager's bonus for a given year would be the result of that year's performance and the previous two years' performance. For the time being, the company has decided to keep the one-year focus for the cash bonus system and use other long-term incentive programs to keep management focused on the years ahead.

Rose points out that senior management is well aware that some acquisitions and other large investments can depress CVM for the first year or two. For example, when Pinesol was acquired several years ago for $465 million, CVM went down, but it has increased substantially since then. Managers may just have to be confident and patient enough to make decisions in one year that will benefit CVM several years hence—assuming they remain in their assignments long enough to realize the rewards.

Rose believes that CVM is a more useful measure of business performance over time than for a single year. Thus, she discourages managers from using CVM as a decision-making tool. "Managers should not be reluctant to make investments because of the impact on next year's CVM," Rose says. "Rather, they should continue to use net present value for investment decisions."

Another potential problem with CVM, according to Jake Karmendy, Director of Finance, Corporate Staff Functions, is that a manager may decide to overdeliver in a given year, exacting a penalty in the following year. For example, a manager who is on target to meet defined objectives for the year may decide to exceed those objectives to earn a 200 percent bonus. A promotion could be run near the end of the year that drives up shipment volume, or advertising could be reduced. Both would increase earnings for the year, but at the expense of the next year's results.

While Clorox considers CVM appropriate for most of its businesses, there are exceptions. These include its relatively small Brita water filter business and some of its international operations where it is still building infrastructure. In these cases, the company has defined simpler objectives related to growth and profits.

Once CVM was adopted, management had the task of explaining it to nonfinancial managers. Tandowsky, working with others in the finance and administration function, found a way to do it and to make the process fun. He eschewed the usual "lecture course" as being too dry for a cross-section of operating and staff people and looked for something more experiential and team-oriented. He chose to introduce people to basic financial concepts through a board game in which the "players" put "money" behind their decisions for a manufacturing company. After playing the game, people were introduced to economic value added and CVM. The board game Tandowsky selected for the exercise was produced by a vendor specializing in games related to finance.

Summarizing Clorox's experience in implementing CVM, Rose says,

> We have had very strong brand equities and productive, talented people. As a company, we have always been good at execution. What we needed to do was to point the arrow in the right direction and it's finally happened. Craig Sullivan helped the company define and focus on the right businesses. Once we started managing the right businesses, CVM helped us see what we should be measuring to manage them properly.

Capital Budgeting

The implementation of an economic profit metric has not changed the company's NPV-based capital budgeting procedures. The two methods coexist comfortably. NPV and IRR analyses always have been required for new product investments and for acquisitions. Now, capital expenditures exceeding $5 million must be approved by the CEO. For smaller amounts at the division level, CVM itself helps regulate capital spending.

Clorox uses an 8 percent cost of capital, assuming no inflation. Revenues and costs are projected using constant dollars. It is easier to focus on volume increases, cost reductions, and operating margins when inflationary cost increases are not factored in. Thirty percent debt is assumed, although the company's debt has only once exceeded that level and usually is lower. Figures from Ibbotson's *Stock, Bonds, Bills, and Inflation* yearbook for a 75-year period are used. During that time, equities have returned 6 percent over the risk-free rate to investors. In the past 20 years, the risk-free rate has been higher and the equity premium has been lower.

Rose describes CVM as a mindset and net present value as a decision tool. She believes technical skills in the finance function and financial acumen in the corporation overall have increased substantially during the past several years.

Repurchase of Stock

As Clorox continues to generate more cash than it needs to reinvest in the business, it has a choice of accumulating excess cash on its balance sheet or giving it back to its shareholders. It can return it by either paying dividends or repurchasing stock, driving up the value of each share. The company repurchased $100 million of its stock in 1994, believing that it is more efficient for shareholders to take excess cash in the form of capital gains.

How Investors and Analysts View the Company

It took some time for CEO Sullivan to establish credibility with the analyst community. At his first meeting with analysts in 1992, he said that he and his management team would set priorities and develop a strategy for improving performance and generating a superior return to stockholders. The analysts were skeptical and unenthused. Sullivan then returned with a strategy and explained it very clearly. The analysts listened but reserved their judgment until they could see results. The following year, he reiterated his message and reported that Clorox was continuing to execute its plan and to deliver results. Year by year, the company has continued to build a reputation for consistency and predictability.

People Interviewed

Lloyd P. Chasey, Director, Household Products Division Finance and Accounting

Jake Karmendy, Director of Finance, Corporate Staff Functions

Karen Rose, Vice President and Treasurer

Keith Tandowsky, Director of Finance and Accounting, The Kingsford Products Division

10

E.I. du Pont de Nemours and Co.

Five years ago, DuPont recognized that earnings and cash flow were not meeting targets, so management began a program of divestiture, downsizing, and working smarter. Between 1990 and 1994, the company's total employment dropped from 144,000 to 107,000 jobs. Layers of management were reduced and organizational barriers were eliminated to give people close to the markets the authority to act faster and more decisively. The company eliminated an entire layer of senior management and support staff, and reorganized into 23 SBUs that now report to a five-person office of the chief executive.

Before this reorganization, the company's businesses were grouped into several large sectors, each headed by a senior vice president/department head. Important strategic planning and marketing decisions, including capital investment proposals of more than $5 million, had to be approved by corporate-level executives who were not close to the businesses. Department heads seemed to be evaluated by how much capital they could get. Form seemed to be more important than substance, and the sectors were so large that important business issues were overlooked. For example, nylon, Dacron™, and Lycra™ were all managed in one sector; and though there were marketing synergies, each product was in a different stage of its life cycle and had different competitive challenges and business issues. Cost problems with nylon were hidden by Lycra™ profitability. In all, the business sector bureaucracy created a big distance between corporate management and the business units.

The new structure was designed to enable business units to be more responsive to changes in their markets while being more accountable for financial performance. Vice presidents and general managers are now holistically accountable for their SBUs. They present annual and longer-term plans for approval and periodically review progress and important issues with the office of the chief executive. All but the very largest capital budgeting decisions are made at the SBU level as part of approved business plans.

Financial Performance Metrics

The reorganization called for new ways to measure the financial performance of SBUs as if they were independent businesses. This requirement did not mean a radical change in du Pont's performance measurement systems, just an enhancement.

DuPont's principal financial metrics for evaluating business unit performance are after-tax operting income (ATOI) and components of cash flow not related to financing. Cash from operations, working capital, capital expenditures, and net cash flow after capital expenditures are measured against the plan for each business unit. Management also considers other ratios such as permanent investment turnover (sales divided by permanent investment), the variable margin (sales less variable costs divided by sales), fixed-cost productivity (sales divided by controllable fixed costs), and working-capital turnover. Within working capital the company tracks the number of days of inventory, accounts payable, and accounts receivable.

DuPont considers turnover metrics to be both financial and behavioral. Part of its purpose is to encourage people below the general management level to make the resources they have been entrusted with work harder. Salespeople have to work with credit people and understand that a sale is not a sale until the cash comes in. They have to think about generating more sales with less receivables and inventory.

Recently, the company introduced two new financial performance measures: RONA and shareholder value added (SVA). RONA is defined as ATOI, with no financing charges, divided by net assets. Net assets are total assets (after depreciation) less current liabilities without short-term borrowings. RONA is an improvement over ROE as a profitability ratio because it takes into account management of the entire balance sheet without consideration of external financing. RONA is a measure of return on total capital employed, and is not influenced by the ratio between debt and equity.

SVA, a variant of economic value added, is defined as ATOI minus a capital charge, which is the cost of capital multiplied by net assets. SVA is the dollar value of the spread between RONA and the weighted average cost of capital.

DuPont considers SVA a useful addition because it unites earnings and investment in a single monetary measure of performance. It makes managers more aware of the corporate resources they are using. However, at this point, SVA has no bearing on managers' compensation.

Like any other single metric, SVA has limitations. It is more useful when considered over time than for a single year. It is book based, not cash based. On the other hand, cash-based measures have limitations as well, particularly because cash flow in any one year can give a distorted picture of performance.

While DuPont is aware that SVA creates value by generating cash flow over time, the company is equally concerned about measuring performance in every time period. The accrual-based SVA measure allows people not specialized in finance to understand the dynamic of creating value. It conveys this message: "You are obliged to earn on the capital invested in your business and to repay that capital over time." Charles Cantwell, financial consultant, believes there is a danger in the way some people think about sunk costs. "They think that what they spent yesterday doesn't matter and that only what they earn tomorrow is important." They forget about the millstone around their necks called "previously spent capital" that must generate a continuing return and be repaid as well. Through a capital charge, SVA continually reminds managers of their obligation to earn on capital already on the ground.

Measuring Managers' Performance

ATOI and cash flow are the primary focus for evaluating the performance of vice presidents and general managers. How the general managers use SVA, RONA, and other measures within their business units is up to them. They generally will use SVA as one of their measures for the top level of managers reporting to them. Beyond that, measures are not standardized because businesses have different growth characteristics, market dynamics, and demands in meeting customer needs. du Pont's businesses range from agricultural chemicals with fairly high margins to fibers with high volume and low margins. Each business establishes goals and performance objectives for the year based on its unique circumstances. Managers' objectives are to deliver on those plans.

Business-Unit Financial Statements

An important part of implementing the SVA measure is producing more accurate and complete business-unit balance sheets. In the past, DuPont's business units had limited balance sheets, and many assets and liabilities were classified as "corporate." Now the company is assigning as many of those corporate items to the business units as it can, eliminating a large "all other" category that in the past was too easy for people to consider someone else's problem. Working capital items have been relatively easy to allocate. Assets such as the main DuPont office building in Wilmington, Delaware, other office facilities, shared investments in staff functions, capitalized interest, and other corporate assets, along with current liabilities such as taxes payable and other postemployment benefits (e.g., health care for retirees) have had to be allocated by formula in the most reasonable way possible.

Adjustments to Earnings and Capital

Some companies make substantial adjustments to their reported figures to put earnings and capital on an economic basis, but DuPont prefers to keep things simple, making as few adjustments as possible. Property, plant, and equipment at the SBU level is in line with externally reported numbers; it is not adjusted for current or replacement value. When assets are eliminated, the amount of capital invested declines by the book value of those assets, so disposal of fully depreciated assets has no effect on an SBU balance sheet. When management is comparing business-unit performance, it knows to take into account that book numbers do not reflect replacement values, and older businesses may appear to have relatively high RONA ratios because their assets have depreciated. Most of DuPont's businesses reinvest so consistently that their total net assets do not diminish much over time.

DuPont believes that the SVA measure will be most helpful when it can be used to measure the progress of its businesses over time. Right now, it has only a couple of years of full financial data based on the current SBU organizational structure. Reconstruction of the data going back would be a monumental task for such a big company, and the numerous adjustments required could cause confusion and credibility problems for managers being judged by the numbers.

How Finance Function Works with Business Units

DuPont's finance function is well integrated into the businesses. It takes the lead in developing financial performance measures used throughout the corporation and in helping managers develop additional measures appropriate to their businesses. Only four core financial activities are considered corporate: treasury, audit, tax, and corporate accounting. (Corporate accounting pulls together the data for external reporting.) Credit support, financial planning, control, and other financial functions are within business units. Accounting, though centralized, assigns people to work directly with each unit.

Each SBU has a financial manager who is in effect the CFO and part of the business leadership team. These managers report to both the business unit head and John Jessup, Vice President and Controller. This dual reporting relationship helps them become part of the business units and maintain their finance function identities. The finance leadership group, consisting of the SBU financial managers, has been involved with implementation of the SVA measurement system as well as the balance sheet project.

Cantwell has seen a real behavior change in the finance function in the 15 years he has been with the company. "Finance people used to ask line people for data and require them to prepare budgets and maintain records. Now they help line people and work with them as part of a team effort."

Financial Reporting System

DuPont has what it calls a global financial database that is accessible to people who need it, and allows information to be assembled in virtually any way. Within the system there is a full earnings statement, full cash-flow statement, and a balance sheet for each SBU. To track performance, business managers and analysts can go down to any level within a business unit, download the information they consider most useful, and present it however they want.

Capital Budgeting Procedures

DuPont uses net present value analysis for almost all investment decisions. The adoption of economic-profit-based performance metrics has not changed its capital budgeting procedures. Cantwell considers the two measures compatible, noting that discounted economic value added is equal to NPV. The principal noncash charge in DuPont's SVA measure is depreciation, which in combination with the capital charge corresponds over time to the cash outflow in a net present value calculation. These charges are analogous to a home mortgage—depreciation corresponding to the principal repayment and the capital charge corresponding to the interest.

Most capital expenditures are approved within business units as part of their approved business plans. Only the largest require approval at the corporate level. The company has published guidelines for project proposals, including a suggested format and information that should be included. Those guidelines suggest minimum requirements such as a net present value analysis, but they are not meant to be straitjackets. There are big differences among joint ventures, "greenfield" plants, cost-savings projects, and environmental projects, and proposals differ accordingly.

Capital investment requests are written in layman's language. They generally include a discussion of how the new investment will fit into the business's overall strategy; what alternatives were considered in developing the investment plan; what the most important uncertainties are; what contingency plans and alternative time frames exist; and a summary of project economics expressed in terms of NPV, IRR, **discounted payback**, and the profitability index. The discounted payback is the time that elapses until the project has a positive net present value. The profitability index is the **present value** of cash inflows from operations divided by the present value of investment outflows. The expected NPV for a project is calculated for the total project life; for periods during the course of the project such as construction, the first five years, and the second five years; and for the project's terminal value. This approach focuses attention on when the project is expected to generate most of its value and which assumptions need the most critical scrutiny.

Key uncertainties for the project are identified, and a range of possible outcomes is quantified for each uncertainty over the range of 10 to 90 percent probability. For example, a business may believe that there is a 10 percent chance of selling 10 million units or more, a 50 percent chance of selling 8 million units or more, and a 90 percent chance of selling 7 million units or more. Other uncertainties in the analysis might include project cost, raw material prices, product selling prices, market share, and market growth. The effect that each variable could have on the project is quantified assuming all other variables are held at the 50 percent probability level. The NPV impact of individual uncertainties can be illustrated by graphing NPV for 10, 50, and 90 points. For example, in Figure 10-1 a plant expansion project has a NPV of $6.5 million, assuming that each of the five variables is at the 50 percent probability level, and thus there is an equal chance that actual results will be above or below the median. But values on either side of the median will not necessarily be the same. While no single uncertainty is likely to cause a negative NPV, results for this project are highly sensitive to market factors such as selling prices and market share.

FIGURE 10-1 NPV Sensitivity to Uncertainties

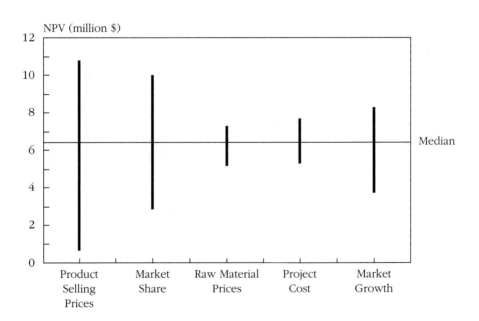

Managers are encouraged not to think that the best and worst cases are simply 10 or 20 percent above or below the median, but rather to capture a full 80 percent of the total uncertainty. Their upside estimates may be more optimistic than their downside, or vice versa, and part of Figure 10-1's purpose is to show the skew of the distribution. In this figure, there appears to be somewhat more downside risk, especially in selling prices.

Range of Outcomes

For the most critical uncertainties, probability distributions are assessed, and cumulative probability distributions of NPV and profitability index are developed. Monte Carlo simulations or decision trees are used to develop these curves. Figure 10-2 shows a range of NPV outcomes. Figure 10-3 shows a range of profitability index outcomes. Similar charts are included in the company's capital investment requests.

FIGURE 10-2 Range of NPV Outcomes

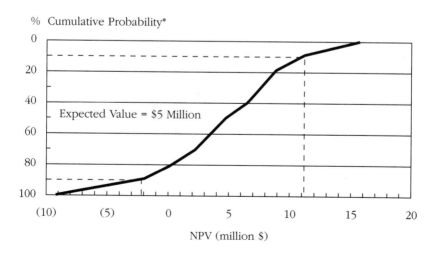

*Probability that outcome will be this favorable or better.

FIGURE 10-3 Range of Profitability Index Outcomes

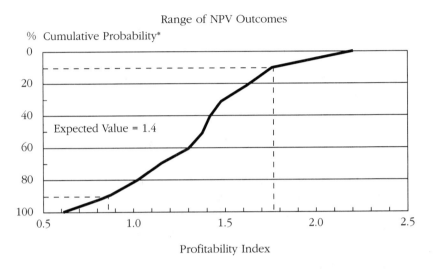

*Probability that outcome will be this favorable or better.

Decision and Risk Analysis

For large decisions, including projects of more than $5 million, DuPont frequently uses an analytical procedure called decision and risk analysis (D&RA). This process builds on the analytical techniques discussed earlier under "Capital Budgeting Procedures" to help managers consider alternative strategies, analyze uncertainties, make decisions, and develop implementation plans in a particularly rigorous way.

Typically, the analysis is performed by a multifunctional project team and overseen by a multifunctional decision board. The project team creates strategy tables (Figure 10-4) to display the most important decision alternatives in categories such as manufacturing, technical development, and sales and marketing. It develops influence diagrams (Figure 10-5) showing how all the uncertainties relate to each other and how they impact net present value. Before proceeding with the quantitative analysis, the team reviews this framework with the decision board. The project team then does in-depth analysis of marketing, manufacturing, and technical uncertainties, consulting subject matter experts, usually

FIGURE 10-4 Sample Strategy Table

Strategy	Manufacturing — Location: Europe/Americas	Manufacturing — Location: Asia/Pacific	Other Manufacturing Issues	Technical Development	Sales & Marketing — Market Segment	Sales & Marketing — Pricing
Base case	Convert quality worth and/or relative worth to batch	Flexible batch	X products + batch	Develop/install batch process	Diversity from construction	Regional parity
	Shutdown quality worth or relative worth		Y products	Increase technical staff 10%	Focus on high value-in-use	Strategic price (region/segment only)
	No change	Group finishing	JIT manufacturing - All - Pretreat only	Decrease technical staff 25%	Limited line/ high-volume applications	Industry segment (multitier)
		No change	Optimize task for capacity	No change technical staff	Grow segment A	Full-book
Product differentiation	Flexible, low cost pretreat	Flexible, low cost pretreat	Optimize task for inventory	Drive breakthrough products—new technology	Pretreat WW	High price - Selected product - Low priority markets
	Group finishing		Buy/resell	Consolidate technical service 1 lab/region	Create new markets + 2 market development people	Competitive pricing
Cost leadership	Eliminate foaming		Reduce emissions 10%/year	New products to match competition		
				Remove tars		

FIGURE 10-5 Sample Influence Diagram

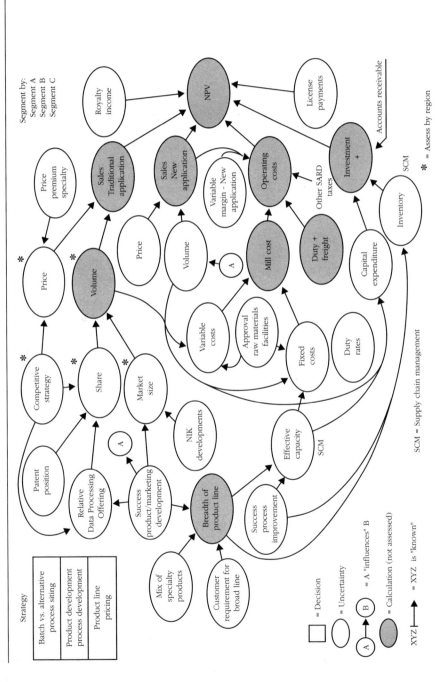

within the company. These data enable the project team to analyze what is creating value for a business and what is generating the most uncertainty. Following a review of the analysis with the decision board, the project team develops implementation plans including action steps, measures to minimize risk, contingency planning, metrics to measure progress, and required cultural changes. These plans are then reviewed at a subsequent decision-board meeting.

DuPont believes that the decision and risk analysis process has enhanced team building, increased the level of attention paid to new and different strategic approaches, and created buy-in and commitments to major decisions.

Cost of Capital

DuPont's weighted average cost of capital is 12 percent. This figure is used as the discount rate for net present value analysis in all the business units. Management considers businesses healthy if they have 14 percent or higher RONA. That number is higher than the cost of capital in order to cover corporate items, and also because management wants people to strive to earn more than the cost of capital. Cantwell acknowledges that companies can get very involved in computing and updating their WACC and in ascribing different costs of capital to different business units based on risk, comparable companies in the same industries, and so forth. But he believes that 12 percent serves the company's measurement needs well and is not far off the mark. He does not think that fine-tuning the cost of capital would be in the company's best interest.

Financial Structure

Performance metrics such as SVA have little bearing on DuPont's capital structure. The company manages its capital structure so that debt will be at a comfortable level, providing operating and financial flexibility without jeopardizing the company's debt rating. DuPont did not take on any debt until the late 1960s. Now it is not afraid of leverage when appropriate. It used substantial debt financing to buy Conoco and some debt to buy back Seagram's interest in the company but has been working its leverage back to a level it considers normal.

How Investors and Analysts Value the Company

DuPont's management believes that investors buy its stock for total return—a combination of price appreciation and dividends. The company's current TSR target is 15 percent. The TSR target is higher than the WACC because of modest leverage. du Pont's dividend yield is currently 3.2 percent, and over time it has generally stayed in the range of 3 to 3.5 percent. DuPont has been reasonably successful in exceeding the S&P 500.

Cantwell sees more discussion of price-earnings ratios and price-to-cash-flow ratios than evidence of DCF analysis in sell-side security analysts' reports, but he believes that those who use short-term ratios generally understand the longer-term cash-flow dynamics. The story du Pont shares with the market is one of growth in earnings and, in turn, growth in cash flow over time.

Analysts sometimes value DuPont and other large industrial companies by the amount of their capital expenditures and whether there appears to be a corresponding improvement in cash flow over time. Several years ago, one Wall Street firm criticized DuPont for getting insufficient cash back for all the capital it was investing. Now there are more comments that the company is controlling its capital expenditures and getting good returns. That opinion seems to be reflected in a recent improvement in the company's stock price.

Short- and Long-Term Perspective

DuPont pays attention to short-term as well as long-term results. Cantwell believes that very few public companies are unconcerned with short-term earnings results, but he does not think DuPont would make a decision to bolster quarterly results that would be damaging to the long-term health of the business. Sheer size helps the company offset businesses that are investing in future growth with businesses that are generating substantial cash returns. When businesses are in a heavy investment mode, their financial metrics are expected to reflect it, and the reasons for relatively low short-term returns are taken into account in evaluating their managers. If DuPont made an acquisition of the magnitude of Conoco, and that investment depressed earnings and ratios in the short term, the company would communicate to investors why it expected such an investment to create value in the longer term.

People Interviewed

Charles W. Cantwell, Manager, Special Studies—Packaging and
     Industrial Polymers
John P. Jessup, Vice President Finance and Controller
John C. Sargent, Vice President and Treasurer

11

Federal Signal Corporation

Federal Signal Corporation is a manufacturer and worldwide supplier of safety, signaling, and communications equipment; fire trucks; rescue vehicles; street sweeping and vacuum loader vehicles; parking control equipment; custom on-premise signage; carbide cutting tools; precision punches; and related die components. Founded in 1901, the firm does some $800 million in sales annually. Federal Signal has four major operating groups—safety products, sign, tool, and vehicle—and has a decentralized management approach. The company's strategy is to maintain a leading position through innovative product development and superior operating performance in low-technology niche markets. It believes that a company with the number-one position in an industry can command a premium price and act as a market leader in addition to benefiting from economies of scale. Ninety-eight percent of the company's 1994 domestic sales were in markets in which it held the number-one market share. Now the company is expanding into more international markets. Sales to foreign buyers increased from 8 percent of total sales in 1988 to 19 percent in 1994.

Federal Signal has invested more than $200 million to acquire 19 companies in the last decade. The company believes that its diversity helps maintain consistent earnings growth, but it does not consider itself a conglomerate. There is considerable marketing synergy within each group. While group and division presidents have substantial autonomy, the company culture encourages them to work together and share ideas on manufacturing and marketing wherever possible. Joe Ross, Chairman and CEO, gives a "white hat" award each year to the division which has not only demonstrated outstanding performance under operating and financial metrics, but also has helped build the company's overall management infrastructure.

The company maintains low leverage, a thin corporate staff, and tight control over spending. Total debt to capitalization for manufacturing operations at the end of 1994 was 22 percent. There are 25 people on the corporate staff in Oak Brook, Illinois, 11 of whom are in finance. Even with an emphasis on product development and innovation, the company makes relatively modest capital expenditures each year, which are covered several times by cash flow from operations. Strict cost control starts at the top. There are few individual subscriptions to the *Wall Street Journal,* and everyone, including the chairman, flies coach on both domestic and international flights.

Financial Metrics

Federal Signal's two most important financial objectives are a 15 percent average increase in annual earnings per share over time and a 20 percent ROE. Management considers the achievement of the company's financial goals to be rooted in basic operating performance. Therefore, it also pays close attention to the operating margin, working capital, and other asset utilization ratios.

At the business-unit level, the ROE metric in effect is a RONA metric. For performance measurement purposes, capital invested in a business is defined as total assets minus non-interest-bearing current liabilities. Items on the corporate balance sheet such as debt, pension liabilities, and other nonoperating accrued liabilities are excluded from the business unit's balance sheet. The only balance sheet item that business-unit managers cannot control is goodwill, and there has been some debate within the company about whether it should be included.

Federal Signal has used performance measures such as operating margins and inventory turns for decades. Strategic objectives cascade into a valuation model and operating parameters to guide people in sales, manufacturing, and other functions throughout the company. Questions addressed include the following: How can we maximize value? Where do we go for sales growth? How risky is each new market? How do we prioritize? Each component of inventory is carefully managed. Finished goods relate to customer service. Work in progress relates to the manufacturing cycle. Raw materials involve clever purchasing, making sure suppliers stick to delivery schedules, and perhaps partnering with suppliers.

In the mid-1980s, the company decided that the best way to create value was to capitalize on its leading market positions, improve margins, and reduce working capital. Between then and 1994, Federal Signal improved its operating margin from 7 percent to more than 11 percent and reduced working capital from 27 percent to 10 percent of sales.

Federal Signal is often just as concerned with year-over-year performance as it is with the absolute value of a business. It uses its accumulated expertise to improve the margins of newly acquired companies. The vehicle group's operating margin slipped from 10.5 percent in 1993 to 9 percent in the second quarter of 1995 as it folded in the operations of Vactor Manufacturing, the leading U.S. manufacturer of municipal catch basin and sewer cleaning equipment, and Guzzler Manufacturing, the leading U.S. supplier of industrial cleaning trucks. But the vehicle group saw opportunities to improve manufacturing efficiency and combine marketing operations for similar products and expects to double the operating margins of the newly acquired companies in the near future.

Now that the company's base businesses have largely reached their margin improvement goals, Federal Signal is putting greater emphasis on growth—taking its existing strengths into new markets abroad. The company is already the world's leading producer of fire engines and street sweepers. It plans to expand its international market share of those and other products.

Duane Doerle, Director of Corporate Development, has helped business-unit managers identify complementary markets peripheral to the markets they currently serve. For example, the Tool Group, which makes punches and dies for metal stamping, has good margins but is not growing fast enough. It has a good market position within a broad group of metal working manufacturers but has a lot of room to grow in other industrial markets such as beverage can tooling, where it has only a 10 percent market share.

Management wants businesses to grow their top lines even if doing so reduces their margins somewhat. This emphasis represents a new paradigm for managers who have worked over the years to improve margins. They are learning that substantial sales generating returns 3 percent above the cost of capital can create more value than modest sales generating 5 percent above the cost of capital.

Henry Dykema, Vice President and Chief Financial Officer, observes that as businesses grow and change, they excel in some areas while developing their skills in others. A business with highly developed skills in cost cutting and working-capital management can initially find the sales-growing process more difficult. Developing global markets requires different skills that take time to develop.

Doerle has used a valuation model to help each business identify growth opportunities. He does sensitivity tests that allow him to compare the benefits that can be gained from improvements in margins, working-capital reduction, and growth. He can help managers pinpoint businesses where there is relatively little value to be gained from further margin improvement and greater value to be gained from growth. He also can calculate the effects of various sales levels and margins, giving managers comfort that they will not destroy value by reducing margins to increase sales.

Valuation Model

Doerle uses the discounted cash-flow model to value the company's existing businesses and prospective acquisitions. He does sensitivity analyses to see the effect of variables such as margins, growth, and the level of payables, receivables, and inventory on the value of each business. He projects annual cash flows for five years, or longer if a business strategy calls for it. At the end of that period, he uses a growth perpetuity that assumes that free cash flow will continue to grow at 3 or 4 percent per year for Federal Signal businesses and a more conservative 2 percent for potential acquisitions. By using a growth perpetuity, he avoids the highly variable method of estimating a terminal value using market comparables. The company considers its growth perpetuity assumptions conservative. It has had good experience using these assumptions coupled with **sensitivity analysis** and other "pluses and minuses" in its valuation work.

For many of Federal Signal's businesses and acquisitions, Doerle estimates capital spending by keeping the model's fixed assets at a certain percentage of sales. He uses more specific information on capital spending plans if good estimates can be made. In valuing a target company, Doerle works with a team from the operating group that is considering the acquisition. Together they develop assumptions on combination benefits in both manufacturing and marketing, fixed capital investments that would be required, or how the pattern of capital spending might change under Federal Signal's management. Over the years, virtually all of the operating managers have worked with Doerle on acquisitions and become familiar with the company's valuation methodology.

Doerle uses Federal Signal's weighted average cost of capital as a discount rate for all capital budgeting and valuation. The company does not use different discount rates for different businesses because it is difficult to get the information to do it properly, and best estimates are always subject to question. Doerle's cost-of-capital worksheet is shown in Figure 11-1. He gets the premium for the cost of common equity over the 30-year Treasury rate from Ibbotson's *Stocks, Bonds, Bills, and Inflation*. To calculate Federal Signal's cost of equity, he multiplies that premium by Federal Signal's beta and adds the resulting figure to the 30-year Treasury bond rate. The cost of debt is a blended rate with components varying from short-term to 10-year debt rates. He then calculates a WACC reflecting Federal Signal's target mix of 70 percent equity and 30 percent debt based on book values.

FIGURE 11-1 Cost-of-Capital Worksheet

Cost of equity
   Premium (Ibbotson study)   5.6%
   Federal Signal *beta* (leveraged)   times   _____
   Subtotal   _____
   30-year Treasury rate   plus   _____
   Cost of equity   _____

Cost of debt
   Blended rate   _____
   Tax rate   _____
   After-tax cost of debt   _____

Cost of capital
   70% (cost of equity) + 30% (after-tax cost of debt)
   0.7 (   ) + 0.3 (   )
   _____   _____

   _____

The target debt level is high enough to reduce the company's cost of capital but not so high as to create unnecessary financial risk. If the company were to use its actual debt-to-equity ratio in its cost-of-capital calculation, its cost of capital would rise as debt was paid down because equity is more expensive than debt. Consequently the company's hurdle rate, the WACC, is based on the targeted rather than the actual debt-to-equity ratio. It is management's responsibility to make sure that the actual debt-to-equity ratio never gets too far from the target. This can be done by funding acquisitions with debt, increasing dividends, buying back company stock, or using a combination of these options.

The valuation model is a useful tool for both acquisitions and strategic planning. Doerle discusses different assumptions with business managers and often does 20 or 30 different scenarios. For example, what if you grow sales by an additional 1 percent per year? What if you adopt an aggressive pricing strategy to grow market share? What if you improve margins by 0.5 percent? What are the real value drivers? Could a strategy that looks good on the surface turn out to be a value killer? Tweaking the numbers gives him a feel for each business.

Dykema comments that business managers have become increasingly comfortable with using net present value analysis in their strategic planning. They feel that they now have a tool to translate their operating strategies into financial parameters that the CEO needs. Before these types of models were used for strategic planning, they had to rely on forecasted income statements and balance sheets, which usually predicted poor returns on capital projects in the initial years. They did not have a tool to give them confidence that they were creating value.

Capital Budgeting

Capital spending constraints based on borrowing capacity have not been a problem for Federal Signal. The challenge has been to get business managers to come up with more new proposals to grow their businesses.

For capital budgeting analysis, the company prefers IRR calculations to NPV calculations because it likes to compare a project's IRR with its level of risk. A low-risk project, such as new equipment for which cost savings can be estimated accurately, might require an IRR only 2 percent above the company's 10 percent WACC. A higher-risk project, such as developing a new product or entering a new market, generally requires a higher IRR. Doerle works with managers to do sensitivity analyses for many large capital budgeting proposals, working out best and worst case scenarios and seeing how the IRR changes as various assumptions are changed. If the IRR drops radically based on conservative assumptions, then the project is considered risky.

Incentive Compensation

Compensation for division presidents has three components: salary, cash bonus, and a combination of stock awards and options. The CEO makes the decisions. Stock awards and options are discretionary. Cash bonus target tables are set annually. About 15 percent of cash bonuses are based on corporate performance and the remaining 85 percent on subsidiary or group performance, depending on the manager's span of control. The subsidiary or group performance part is based on how well presidents have carried out their strategic plans, how the performance of their businesses has improved over the past several years, how difficult their plans have been to achieve, and how well they have attended to key value drivers such as sales growth. Priorities for the coming year for each group are worked out by the chairman, the CFO, and the controller and negotiated with the group presidents. This year for the first time, the company is using a matrix for certain operating groups that defines a bonus level for each combination of sales growth and operating margin. The matrix will provide two benefits: it will help managers see how various growth and return targets create value, and it will add objectivity to the bonus plan.

Below the group president level, direct reports (e.g., vice presidents of finance, operations, or engineering) generally have compensation plans based partly on the group plan submitted to the chairman and partly on their own specific goals. Days sales outstanding might be one of the measures for the vice president of finance, and inventory turnover might be a measure for the vice president of operations. Also, group presidents sometimes define bonus plans for all employees based on group profits.

Division presidents have the discretion (subject to approval of the CEO or board of directors) to recommend cash and stock option programs for their own staff members at all levels. A total of 13 percent of the company's stock is held by 60 percent of Federal Signal employees.

How Investors and Analysts
View the Company

Federal Signal has provided annual compounded TSRs of 26 percent during the 5 years ending in 1994 compared with 9 percent for the S&P's Mid-Cap 400 Index list, and 22 percent during the past 15 years compared with 11 percent for the S&P Mid-Cap 400. Its average annual earnings-per-share growth has been 16 percent over the past 5 years and 13 percent over the past 15 years. The company has a track record of steady performance as evidenced by a beta of less than one. If the company continues to meet its stated goals of 15 percent average EPS growth, it will roughly double in size every 5 years.

Dykema believes that the company's performance record and its consistent strategy have created high credibility with investors and analysts. The company generates increasing cash flow consistent with its increase in earnings over time and knows how to invest in continued growth, both internally and in the purchase of related businesses. It has proven skills in improving the margins of companies it acquires.

Just over half of Federal Signal's stock is held by institutional investors. Dykema considers this portion surprisingly low, but believes that much of the remaining stock is held by individuals investing for the long term who are attracted by the steady growth rate. Because the company's performance is so steady, Federal Signal sees relatively few momentum investors. Dykema believes that momentum investors look for potential short-term price movements of 20 percent or more.

Valuation with Analysts'
Cash-Flow Estimates

Dykema subscribes to a service that summarizes analysts' earnings and growth estimates. The company can use its DCF model to see if the current price of its stock is consistent with these estimates. Based on the current level of free cash flow, analysts' estimates can be used to grow cash flow for five years and to calculate a growth perpetuity. Doerle thinks a 3 to 4 percent growth rate is appropriate for the growth perpetuity formula, considering 2.5 to 3 percent growth in the economy and Federal Signal's steady history of growth. The WACC is used as a discount rate. The company segments its finance receivables and related debt financing and assigns them a lower cost of capital based on higher leverage.

People Interviewed

Duane Doerle, Director of Corporate Development
Henry L. Dykema, Vice President and Chief Financial Officer
Richard L. Ritz, Vice President and Controller

12

FMC Corporation

FMC is a $4 billion corporation with businesses in five major groups: (1) performance chemicals, including agricultural chemicals, pharmaceutical and food ingredients, process additives, and proprietary products used for biotechnology; (2) industrial chemicals; (3) machinery and equipment, including energy and transportation equipment and food machinery; (4) defense systems; and (5) precious metals, principally gold.

Evolution of Performance Measures

FMC has used several different financial performance metrics over the past two decades. The company's experience reflects some of the strengths and weaknesses of different measurement systems as well as changing economic conditions and FMC's own corporate evolution.

Cash Flow Return on Investment

FMC introduced the proprietary cash flow return on investment (CFROI) model in 1979 and used it in the early 1980s. At that time, the company was a far more diverse conglomerate than it is today. Some of its businesses were capital intensive and some were not. The company needed a way to put businesses on an equal footing to help define an adequate return on capital employed. Inflation was a problem; and replacing decades-old capital assets at 1980 prices was creating measurement difficulties. The CFROI model attempted to adjust for inflation by using an indexing system that inflated assets to current dollar values.

CFROI is an IRR measure. A related spot valuation model starts with the current rate of return on a company's businesses, projects future cash flows based on assumed rates of capital investment and above-average rates of return fading to market norms over time, and discounts the resulting cash flows at a market-derived discount rate. (This methodology is discussed in detail in the National Semiconductor case.) Valuations for businesses are compared with external benchmarks that indicate the value they might hold for other corporate owners. This approach provided former CEO Robert Malott and his team with a new tool to estimate the value of businesses to FMC and the return they should expect from those businesses.

For three years, the strategic planning group and senior management used the CFROI model as part of an analytic process to rationalize the company's portfolio. The model helped FMC's senior management decide which businesses were healthy, which needed to be fixed, and which should be sold. But the model was difficult to roll out into the business units. It was based on a complex IRR model rather than on the traditional P&L model that managers were familiar with. Management tried to translate what it found useful in the CFROI model into an accounting model that was easier to understand. A new measurement system called "net contribution" was developed for incentive-based compensation.

Net Contribution

To determine net contribution, FMC calculated operating profit after tax (sales minus the cost of sales) and then applied a capital charge. Within the cost of sales, depreciation was calculated based on the current cost and economic life of the asset. Different economic lives were assumed for different types of assets, ranging from 3 or 4 years for computer equipment to 25 years for a chemical plant. The cost of capital was divided into inflationary and real portions, and real rate-of-return targets were set. The hurdle rate was raised to cover corporate overhead. Taxes charged were at an effective or marginal tax rate. The returns that FMC expected from its businesses using this method were lower than reported accounting returns because they were calculating real rather than nominal rates.

Operating Profit After Taxes and Working Capital

In the mid-1980s, FMC decided that net contribution reflected a number of factors, such as capital structure, that were beyond business managers' control, particularly in a one-year time frame. The company decided to use two measures for incentive compensation: operating profit after taxes and working capital. The working capital measure helped FMC generate about $400 million cash from working capital reductions over a four-year period.

FMC continued to adjust assets including land for current values, and levy an 8 percent per year capital charge on those assets. The company had land in places such as Princeton, New Jersey, and San Jose, California, that was purchased in the 1940s, had little value on the balance sheet, but had appreciated substantially. Business managers were encouraged to dispose of whatever land they did not need.

In 1984, the company bought back one-third of its shares because it had more cash than it could possibly invest, and the acquisitions market seemed expensive. In 1986, the company recapitalized, increasing leverage and distributing a major dividend to shareholders. By this time, managing the businesses for cash was instilled in the corporate culture.

A couple of years ago, FMC reevaluated its system for asset valuation and decided to stop making adjustments for inflation. The adjusted asset values were not providing useful signals to management; they were no more accurate than the balance sheet values based on historical cost accounting; and in some cases, asset values after inflation adjustment were higher than replacement costs.

Economic Value Added

FMC adopted economic value added with relatively few adjustments because the approach is easy for business managers to understand. Ron Mambu, Corporate Controller, believes that a company has to make a trade-off between the most technically correct model and a model that provides the right signals and direction indicators but is also broadly understood. According to Mambu, "When an organization understands the objective and gets behind it, you just get out of the way and they'll get the job done."

Mambu recognizes that shareholder value is driven by cash flow over the longer term. However, he believes that cash-flow measures can give a distorted picture of operations in any given year because of the timing of items such as tax payments and capital expenditures. The shorter the period, he believes, the more difficult it is to use cash-flow-based performance measures.

Balanced Scorecard

FMC's businesses are assessed using a balanced scorecard of financial and nonfinancial measures. Each of FMC's 25 SBUs develops its own measures. For example, the scorecards for agricultural chemicals and food machinery are very different. Measures that really drive each business are developed in a bottom-up process. They are reviewed with corporate management as part of the planning process and frequently changed as business objectives evolve. The measures are not viewed as a business unit's contract with management, but as benchmarks that motivate business managers to implement their strategic initiatives and provide feedback on how well they are doing.

The balanced scorecard has focused senior management's attention on a number of nonfinancial measures that had little visibility before: market share; patents; new ideas implemented; new products moving from development to availability; sales of new products; cycle times; customer complaints; late deliveries; amount of time to answer customer inquiries; and other measures of quality, innovativeness, and customer satisfaction.

None of these measures overshadows the importance of traditional financial measures such as operating profit margins, capital turnover, return on average capital employed, and working capital. FMC calculates working capital in four components—accounts receivable, inventory, trade payables, and advance payments—and considers these measures most helpful for assessing performance in a quarter, six months, or a year. It considers economic value added to be more valuable over the longer term.

Incentive Compensation

FMC uses economic value added over a three-year time frame for incentive compensation; managers estimate what their businesses are going to do for the next three years, and compensation systems are based on that estimate.

In the past, managers submitted annual budgets for operating profits before taxes that were intended to have a 50-50 chance of being exceeded or not achieved. But some managers were conservative and submitted budgets that really had a 60 or 70 percent chance of being exceeded, because in their perception, the penalty for not meeting the annual budget was greater than the reward for exceeding it. The new system is designed to encourage stretch earnings targets. Management evaluates each division's three-year plans based on their degree of stretch using a scale from zero to three. If the plan is considered a three and the division reaches the earnings target, then management's target bonus is multiplied by three. Based on the plans submitted, management develops a chart for each division indicating the level of earnings that qualifies for a bonus multiplier of zero, one, two, or three, and the slope of the line is intended to encourage stretch targets. For example, the difference in net contribution between a two and a three bonus multiplier might be less than the difference between a one and a two.

Management is aware that a large acquisition may depress earnings in the short term, and that a business such as agricultural chemicals may find opportunities that require higher R&D expenses than the budget calls for. As long as management understands and agrees with the decision, bonuses and promotions are not affected.

Businesses may make acquisitions that are not in their three-year plans and that have the potential to depress earnings in the short run. FMC protects business managers from the short-term consequences of acquisitions in one of two ways: (1) A business may get approval for an acquisition or capital investment based on performance targets, and its annual net contribution targets during the three-year period are adjusted downward. (2) A business might make its net contribution target even after taking an acquisition into account. In this case, earnings above the net contribution target are considered "gravy." Targets are never adjusted upward.

Implementing Economic Value Added

FMC calculates economic value added for each business unit starting with net income and deducting a charge for capital. The following sections describe how the company determines the capital invested in each unit and the hurdle rate.

Capital Invested

Capital employed is primarily working capital excluding bank and term debt, net property plant and equipment, other operating investments, and goodwill. Intangibles other than goodwill are not capitalized. For example, the agricultural chemicals business has substantial R&D expenditures, and although R&D could be considered an important intangible asset on the balance sheet, these expenditures are not capitalized. The amounts charged to the income statement are relatively consistent from year to year. FMC does not think that capitalizing and amortizing these expenditures would help either performance measurement or the matching of revenues and costs.

Cheryl Francis, Vice President and Treasurer, firmly believes that if one of FMC's business units buys a company, it has to earn a return on the purchase price. She also believes that—for performance measurement purposes—goodwill should be included in the capital invested. But she notes that there is a problem the company has not yet resolved: Businesses are charged twice, because the asset is charged with the company's 11.5 percent cost of capital, and goodwill is still charged off over a 15- to 40-year period. A mitigating factor is that as the asset is charged off, less of it is subject to the capital charge.

Inventory for operating units is recorded on a current dollar cost basis. It is converted to LIFO at the corporate level. FMC has a large LIFO reserve.

Hurdle Rate

FMC uses a hurdle rate of 11.5 percent, slightly above its weighted average cost of capital, for all businesses. People have talked about using different hurdle rates and costs of capital for different businesses, but they have never become comfortable with a way to gauge associated risks and determine effective costs for each business that would average out for the corporation as a whole. Mambu thinks that even if different rates were used for different businesses, the rates would all be between 10 and 12 percent. The company prefers consistency and simplicity.

Problems with Economic Value Added

Francis sees two problems with FMC's current economic-value-added measurement system. First, lease expenses are not capitalized on business units' balance sheets, and so it is not always completely clear to managers that leasing is a financing decision, not an investment decision. When a business buys an asset, it is charged at the 11.5 percent hurdle rate for performance measurement purposes. There are plenty of opportunities to lease equipment at a lower rate, but business-unit managers are not allowed to decide whether to lease or buy. When they want an asset, they get approval, and the finance function does the lease-or-buy analysis. Managers can mistakenly believe that they are losing a potential benefit when they are not allowed to make lease-or-buy decisions.

The other problem is the difficulty of evaluating businesses in inflationary economies such as Mexico. When FMC used a real cost of capital and inflated every business unit's assets, Mexico was on the same basis as the United States. Under the current system, Francis recommends some kind of inflationary adjustment to the capital charge. This move would force business managers to think through their pricing and cost structures to make sure they are generating revenues and margins that sufficiently compensate for high risk and high inflation. If a subsidiary were operating independently, its capital charge might reflect the difference in interest rates between the country concerned and the United States. If inflation were 40 percent in Mexico and 7 percent in the United States, a 33 percent inflation charge would be levied. However, that would be too harsh an adjustment for FMC's Mexican subsidiaries, because FMC does not allocate debt and equity to its businesses.

Capital Budgeting

FMC has a disciplined, rigorous analytic routine for capital budgeting analysis. Its businesses calculate an IRR in which the reinvestment rate is the company's WACC. Corporate audits of capital budgeting proposals give the financial analysis high marks but comment that the proposals need more analysis of how market demand, pricing, and operating costs could vary.

Capital expenditures above $2 million must be approved at the corporate level, and expenditures above $5 million must be approved by the board, but a large capital expenditure often calls for a review of the business unit's entire plan with senior management.

In the past, FMC did extensive capital budgeting analysis at the corporate level, including detailed project rankings and five-year capital projections. Now, rather than approving individual capital expenditures, management is more interested in seeing business units develop good strategies. The units are making more investment decisions within the scope of approved business plans. Top management tends to get involved early in the decision process for major capital expenditures, regardless of whether they are approved at the division or corporate level.

Role of the Finance Function

The control function has an important role in developing financial measures, ensuring they are understood and that they represent the results of each operation fairly and accurately. But today, the controller's role goes far beyond financial measurement. Business-unit controllers are helping line managers make strategic decisions and understand the financial results of those decisions. They participate in the entire planning process, assisting with pricing and sourcing decisions and other trade-offs to improve performance.

FMC's division controllers have been encouraged to think like general managers since the late 1970s. Mambu says that when business-unit controllers start losing their functional identity, the process is beginning to work.

Effect of Performance Measures on Financial Structure

The implementation of economic value added has not affected FMC's overall financial structure. Financing decisions generally have no bearing on business units' performance measurements, but if a unit manager is able to find an opportunity for tax-advantaged financing, the unit's P&L shares the benefits. Often these opportunities are found in foreign countries.

Correlation of Performance Measures to Shareholder Value

Francis believes that the correlation of any model with the behavior of stock prices is very difficult to prove empirically. Over the years, she has tried to predict FMC's share prices with several models, but she has not seen convincing results. She observes that people's conclusions about correlations are sometimes driven by their assumptions.

How Investors and Analysts
Value the Company

Francis thinks that basic economics and cash flow of a business ultimately drive stock prices, but she concedes that this view is difficult to prove. She sees analysts using shortcuts such as price-earnings multiples, but thinks that the people who are doing the best fundamental analysis are focused on cash flow.

Behavioral Changes

Mambu believes that the new measurement systems have changed FMC's culture in two important ways. First, they have moved the company away from using the annual budget as a basis for incentive compensation and thus eliminated the gamesmanship from selling next year's budget to management. Now business managers make three-year earnings estimates and they tend to be more optimistic over the longer term and more willing to stretch. Second, the use of nonfinancial measures in the balanced scorecard has made business managers think more broadly and more strategically.

The new financial measures have helped Chairman Robert Burt shape the company and point it in the direction he wants it to go. He wants less internal and more external focus. He wants to see more emphasis on running businesses superbly; globalizing the company's businesses; developing new products and markets; acquiring new businesses in technologies and markets that FMC understands; and getting, developing, and keeping the best people.

Jeff Simoneau, Division Manager of the Packaging and Materials Handling Division, observes, "You can't just go in with new measurement systems by themselves and expect shifts to take place. Nor can you just go in and say, 'We want everybody now to be customer focused, but we are going to measure you based on whether you achieved your profit targets for this year or not.' It has to all fit together, and that is what has happened over the last few years at FMC."

Simoneau can still remember people in the 1980s debating the merits of financial measures such as profit and return on capital, and talking about nonfinancial measures such as maximizing customer satisfaction. Now he can see these measures fitting together in a complete package.

Simoneau sees the new measures motivating people at all levels. He thinks jobs have been enriched because employees are thinking in broader terms and more people are thinking like general managers. Self-directed employee teams now understand the overall goals of their business units and regularly check measures of on-time deliveries and customer satisfaction. He thinks the people who feel most threatened are lower-level supervisors who are uncomfortable being coaches and catalysts rather than bosses.

Simoneau also thinks it is easy for the company to underestimate the amount of training, coaching, education, and selling that is required to make all these measures work. Training has to be considered an investment, not a cost. Management has to put more emphasis on teaching people to be what they can be. Says Simoneau, "Sometimes management jumps the gun and tosses the ball to them too quickly."

Certain measurements always will be needed, Simoneau adds, but sometimes more can be accomplished with good communication. "When people sit down and talk, they get a good understanding of whether the job is getting done or not. There are no surprises that way."

Simoneau thinks that successful managers in the future will be more willing to take calculated risks because there is more incentive to do so. Bonuses used to be predictable; rarely did anyone do really well or really badly. Simoneau believes that the new incentive system with its longer time horizon will reward people more for taking initiative and changing directions, rather than just holding down costs or squeezing out a little more profit. People at FMC used to talk about cost cutting and capital controls, he adds. Now they talk about the market, the customer, and growth.

People Interviewed

Cheryl A. Francis, Vice President and Treasurer
Ronald D. Mambu, Controller
Ruud P. Roggekamp, Director, Capital Markets and Corporate Finance
Jeffrey G. Simoneau, Division Manager, Packaging and Materials
    Handling Division

13

Meredith Corporation

Meredith Corporation publishes books and such magazines as *Better Homes and Gardens* and *Ladies' Home Journal;* operates television stations; and runs a franchise network of real estate brokers that trade on the *Better Homes and Gardens* name. It is just getting out of the cable television business.

The company has a particularly strong position in magazine publishing. *Better Homes and Gardens* has 7.6 million circulation and, combined with *Ladies' Home Journal,* has a 37 percent market share of advertising pages in the "seven sisters" women's magazines, which also include *Family Circle, Good Housekeeping, McCall's, Redbook,* and *Woman's Day.* Despite this strong position, Meredith sees much of its growth opportunities in broadcasting. Magazine publishing is a business that largely finances itself with up-front subscription revenues. Expanding into broadcasting, on the other hand, requires major investments in new stations.

Meredith's different industries require different external financial performance measures. The company benefits by being in both magazine publishing and broadcasting to the extent that advertising dollars can switch from one to the other, but the dual nature of its business can present a valuation challenge to some analysts and investors who are more accustomed to single-industry companies. At the same time, Meredith illustrates the success of using a relatively simple measure, return on equity, to get everyone in the company focused on a five-year performance improvement goal before moving on to a more sophisticated measure such as economic value added. It also illustrates the use of comparative operating performance measures in each industry and recognizes that these metrics are still the fundamental drivers of shareholder value.

Adoption of an ROE Measure

In 1991 and 1992, Meredith restructured and downsized; 1992 was a loss year; and in 1993, the company's ROE was 6.6 percent, excluding special items. Management looked at the media industry and concluded that a return on equity of at least 15 percent was required to be one of the top five companies, and it set a goal of 15 percent ROE by fiscal 1997. The goal was to be achieved through improved operating performance and with no increase in financial leverage.

Milestone goals were set year by year and group by group to mark the company's progress toward 15 percent ROE. Balance sheet budgeting was introduced for the magazine group, for the real estate group, and for each broadcast station. Now, yearly budgets are based on ROE goals. Targets vary by business: broadcasting is expected to achieve returns close to 30 percent and publishing expects returns in the high teens, excluding corporate overhead and nonearning assets such as cash. Each business determines how much sales growth and margin enhancement it needs to reach its yearly ROE targets.

The 15 percent goal has provided an impetus for revenue growth and cost control in all of Meredith's businesses. Financial managers now look harder at asset utilization. Purchasing managers, always mindful of running out of paper and shutting down the press, have reduced excess inventory of paper and promotional materials. The publishing segment has added a number of new magazines. Meredith has invested in the most advanced desktop publishing equipment in response to the ROE goal and changes in industry technology.

The broadcasting segment has increased its advertising revenues, reduced its programming costs, and made a few staff reductions. Nonproducing advertising salespeople have been replaced. For non-prime-time programming, Meredith has reduced its purchase of television shows "off-network" for rerun and increased its purchase of first-run syndicated shows such as *Wheel of Fortune, Jeopardy*, and *Oprah*. When the company buys off-network reruns for a show such as *Seinfeld*, it must pay up front for several years at a time, running a risk that the show will decline in popularity during that period. First-run shows are purchased a year at a time.

The ROE metric and the company's plans for achieving it, business by business, have taught people throughout the company about Meredith's financial objectives and provided them with a focus. Controller Kathy Zehr points out that the majority of people in this business are marketers or journalists who are not always familiar with financial concepts. Three years ago, few people in the operating groups knew what cash flow was. People have now started to tie returns to what has been invested in the business. They have become more conscious of the cost per page and the cost per hour of programming, even though publishing and broadcasting are not often considered to be unit cost businesses. Management wants people to continue to focus on the ROE goal and the ongoing programs established to reach it. The company reached 8.9 percent ROE (adjusted to eliminate special items) the second year of the program and 12.8 percent the third year. ROE was 16.2 percent in 1996, exceeding the 1997 goal.

Considering an Economic-Value-Added Measure

ROE has served as a transitional measure. Larry Hartsook, Vice President—Finance, believes that by 1997, the company will be ready for a new, more complex goal; and an economic-value-added measure is being considered.

Transition to an economic profit measure will be gradual for two reasons. First, it is reasonably complex to explain across the company; and second, it is not expected to tell Meredith anything radically different from what it already knows.

The company already has good working capital controls. It has monthly reports of days accounts receivable and inventory. A person is assigned to watch those measures and help business units reduce them. The number of days accounts receivable is included as a measure in general managers' and sales managers' incentive packages, so this number is indeed watched closely. Zehr admits that advertising receivable collections could always be a little tighter, especially as revenues rise during each business cycle, but the company needs to be sensitive to its paying customers.

New measures are not really required for inventory control. The paper purchasing function reports to Hartsook, and inventory and purchases are monitored daily. Paper inventory is an important measure, but sometimes large quantities are purchased because a price increase is anticipated.

Economic value added will of course bring more attention to the cost of capital, and the company is considering interim measures—such as interest charges in lieu of capital charges for each business unit—to make people more familiar with the concept. Managers are beginning to understand that if a project does not meet the hurdle rate defined for the business, it will not be approved. Zehr says, "If you don't put concepts such as economic value added in simple terms, you're going to blow them away."

One of the most important things that an economic profit measure will do, in Zehr's opinion, is to make people account for past bad investment decisions. "You can't sweep a bad decision under the carpet," she says. "You are forced to improve your performance in the future. You have to earn on your entire investment base."

Hartsook leans toward making as few adjustments as possible to earnings and capital invested in the interest of making a performance measurement system such as economic value added simple and easy for managers to understand. The company will probably add deferred tax and LIFO reserves to capital as equity equivalents at the corporate level and reverse the amortization of goodwill and film payments at the group level.

"Amortization is different from depreciation," Zehr says. "Including a charge for economic depreciation in earnings makes sense because you are really going to have to replace the asset someday. But you wouldn't normally expect a business you pay a premium for to decline in value." That said, she notes that the media will continue to change with advances in technology, and the effect of that change on the value of publishing and broadcasting properties is difficult to estimate. For example, if Meredith bought a magazine such as *TV Guide* or *People*, it might pay close to $1 billion. Whether it would be worth that much in 10 or 20 years depends on factors such as the merging of television and personal-computer-based media and consumer choice between paper-based and electronic magazines.

Incentive Compensation

Meredith has both long-term incentive plans tied to ROE and annual incentive plans tied to earnings and cash flow, but each group uses additional measures important to its business.

In the magazine group, the group president and the group controller are eligible for bonuses based on earnings and operating cash flow. Earnings are a larger component of the performance measure than cash flow. Bonuses for publishing directors and for the editor and publisher of each magazine are tied largely to profits. The advertising director's performance target is a mix between revenues generated and a profit goal. Further down, targets are based on an individual's specific responsibilities, such as revenue generation for an advertising salesperson.

The company uses less discretion in determining its performance packages than it used to. Now managers are given numbers at the beginning of the year that they have to achieve to earn their bonuses. If they do not achieve the numbers, they do not get bonuses.

Valuing the Magazine Business

It is difficult for Meredith to compare itself financially and competitively with other companies because there are no large public companies with the same mix of magazine publishing and broadcasting. Also, many of the largest magazine publishers, such as Hearst and Conde Nast, are private and do not break out operating and financial figures for the women's magazines that compete with Meredith's.

Magazine publishing and broadcasting businesses are sometimes valued in different ways. Magazine publishers are valued on revenues and earnings, though some analysts capitalize cash flows. Broadcast businesses are measured primarily on cash flow. In Meredith's case, some analysts value its two businesses separately and compute a breakup value.

The most important operating financial measures in magazine publishing are advertising and subscription revenues, along with paper, postage, editorial, production, and subscription acquisition expenses. Meredith's balance in revenues has shifted in recent years from 55 percent subscription revenues and 45 percent advertising revenues to 55 percent advertising and 45 percent subscription. Advertising is a greater percentage of revenues for large-circulation magazines such as *Better Homes and Gardens,* but subscription revenues are a greater percentage for smaller, special interest magazines. The success of a new magazine is measured by acceptance in the advertising community and subscription renewal rates, particularly in the second and third years. Start-up expenses for new magazines are substantial and only partially funded by subscription fees paid up front. The promotion expense for a new magazine is higher than the internal development expense. The peak loss is typically in the first year, and the cumulative breakeven point might not come until the third or even the fourth year.

The best available comparative information for the magazine industry is *The Magazine Handbook*, an annual book of statistics published by the Magazine Publishers Association, the largest of the magazine industry groups. Statistics are also reported to the Publisher's Information Bureau and published in *Advertising Week*, the major magazine trade publication. All of the major publishers contribute information for *The Magazine Handbook*; statistics are shown for different groups of magazines based on circulation levels such as less than one million, more than one million, and more than five million. The identities of the contributors are anonymous. Meredith can tell where *Better Homes and Gardens* ranks under each measure, but it is not able to find the operating margin for a competitor such as *Redbook*.

Among the important comparative measures are market share, editorial costs per page, paper costs per page, and discounts from standard per-page advertising rates. Meredith is interested in the combined market share of *Better Homes and Gardens* and *Ladies' Home Journal* among the seven sisters. Those two publications give Meredith as a company the largest market share in the seven sisters group. The rate card might say $180,000 for a full-page, four-color advertisement in *Better Homes and Gardens*, but discounts offered in the industry might cut that rate by as much as one-half depending on the amount of advertising a customer does.

Cash flow in the magazine business is a continuing cycle of spending money to sell subscriptions, receiving subscription revenues up front, spending money to produce the magazine, and receiving advertising revenues. For instance, *Better Homes and Gardens* sends out large promotional mailings for two-year subscriptions every other year to keep circulation growing. It receives revenues up front, largely in the form of $18 two-year subscription fees.

In the past, Meredith amortized both subscription revenues and promotion expense over the life of magazine subscriptions. It considered earnings and cash flow to even out over about a two-year period. Now, as a result of a recent accounting change, promotion expenses must be recognized when they are incurred, while subscription revenues continue to be deferred. Hartsook believes that earnings and cash flow will once again even out over a cycle, but the question is how long that cycle will be.

Valuing the Broadcasting Business

Broadcasting is an operating-cash-flow margin business, and Meredith uses this measure to compare its operations with other companies. Broadcasting companies are sometimes valued at multiples of operating cash flow. An important difference between net income and operating cash flow in broadcasting is that film acquisition expenses are capitalized and amortized for calculation of net income, but only actual cash payments made for films are recognized when operating cash flow is calculated. Operating cash flow is revenue minus operating expenses; operating expenses include actual cash payments for film but exclude depreciation and the amortization of film payments, goodwill, and other items. Now that the company has moved away from off-network programming and toward first-run programming, it has reduced its up-front payments for films and film amortization.

Meredith compares its broadcast stations with other stations in terms of sign-on-to-sign-off ratings (a station's ratings compared with other stations' ratings between its sign-on and sign-off times); sign-on-to-sign-off advertising market share; and revenue per market share (the amount of revenue it earns for each percentage of market share). It looks at film costs per day part. (The day is divided into parts such as early morning, midmorning, and prime time.) This measure is usually just an internal one, because not much comparative data are available for other companies, but Meredith is able to share information such as operating ratios with other broadcast companies in some local markets.

Regardless of the metrics commonly used in publishing and broadcasting, Hartsook would rather see analysts value Meredith based on projected free cash flow as some are doing. He believes that the best analysts are more interested in EBITDA, as opposed to earnings per share. EBITDA is a useful comparative operating measure and when adjusted for required capital expenditures, represents free cash flow for valuation purposes. Analysts often talk about EPS and price-earnings multiples to retail brokers because that is what brokers want to hear.

Decision to Exit Cable TV Business

Performance measures in the cable television business include percentage penetration of customers who could buy the service and the percentage of customers who subscribe to tiers of channels beyond the basic service.

Meredith recently decided to sell its cable television properties because the economics of the business favor the largest competitors, and cash-flow patterns are not consistent with those of the company's other businesses. When Meredith first decided to get into cable television, the business was unregulated. The company saw an opportunity to increase penetration in selected underutilized markets such as Minneapolis. Then the industry became regulated and prices were rolled back. The economics of the cable business moved toward larger companies that can spread programming costs over a large number of subscribers and receive volume discounts from content providers.

The other problem was negative earnings despite positive cash flow. Cable companies often have heavy depreciation expenses and negative earnings because they are constantly spending money laying new cable and hooking up new subscribers. Also, as the industry consolidates, the largest cable companies are paying premiums over book value to acquire other companies. The amortization of goodwill further depresses their earnings. As a result, many large cable companies report negative income in most years. Zehr thinks that cable TV companies are measured on cash flow partly as a matter of necessity. Accounting-based earnings for the largest players in the business have been so bad that there has been no better way to measure them.

For Meredith, negative earnings accentuated the problem of being in one business that is evaluated more on earnings and another that is evaluated more on cash flow. Net income is still very important to Meredith because the majority of its revenues are in publishing, and its investors tend to be interested in earnings as well as cash flow. Eliminating the earnings drag from the cable television business has been one more step toward achieving the 15 percent ROE goal.

Capital Budgeting and Acquisition Analysis

Meredith usually values potential broadcast station acquisitions in two ways. It estimates cash flows for five years and a terminal value at the end of five years. It also discounts projected broadcasting cash flows over 40 years. Zehr observes that discount rates between 11 and 12 percent are currently used in the industry, and she uses several discount rates to get a range of values. Her revenue projections are based on the target station's current performance; how Meredith believes it can improve that performance; and various statistics such as household growth, retail growth, and cable subscriber growth that help the company esti-mate revenue growth in each designated market area (DMA). The CEO and the COO approve all investment proposals of $100,000 and above. Meredith expects a minimum 15 percent IRR for most invest-ment proposals except for broadcast station acquisitions, which must be lower for competitive reasons. This rate represents a premium over its weighted average cost of capital, which is a little over 10 percent assum-ing 30 percent debt. The company does not want to look at investments that just barely exceed its cost of capital. The cost of equity capital is considered to be a 6 percent premium over the cost of Treasury bills.

A capital budgeting proposal for equipment such as a television camera would be approved based on a net present value analysis of projected cost savings. A proposal for adding a newscast would be ap-proved based on a projected increase in market share and revenues. The company has a revenue estimate for a given level of market share and can therefore estimate the increase in revenues that would result from a given increase in market share.

The Role of the Finance Function

Each business has a group controller responsible for all financial activi-ties except for cash management, which is centralized. Group control-lers handle such functions as business-unit performance analysis, budgeting, accounts receivable collection, and inventory management.

The role of finance people is evolving. Says Hartsook, "There's no question at Meredith that we're business partners." Either Hartsook or Zehr participates in virtually all strategic decisions, evaluates all acquisi-tions, and regularly attends operating group meetings and monthly per-formance reviews with the president of the company. Meredith does not have room for pure old-fashioned accountants who are not able to think flexibly and strategically.

People Interviewed

Larry D. Hartsook, Vice President—Finance
Kathleen Zehr, Corporate Controller and Assistant Secretary

14

National Semiconductor Corporation

National Semiconductor recently began to use the National Semiconductor Value Model (NSVM), which is based on CFROI, to better align its strategic planning with the creation of shareholder value.

In the late 1980s, National Semiconductor's stock price ranged from $23 to $3. Many quarters of continuing losses convinced the company's board and management that the firm had over-invested and was unable to achieve a return above its real cost of capital. It was thus destroying shareholder value while continuing to grow. Incentive compensation plans covering 400 executives were based on half-year financial results and therefore focused on the short term.

In 1991, CEO Charlie Sporck retired after overseeing sales grow from $5 million to $2.5 billion during a 25-year period. Dr. Gilbert Amelio, an engineer and executive with experience at Bell Laboratories, Fairchild Camera and Instrument Corporation, and Rockwell Communications System, became the new CEO. Donald Macleod became CFO shortly thereafter.

National Semiconductor began what it called a corporate transformation: the first phase focused on restructuring; the second phase, begun in 1994, focused on growth. At the beginning of the restructuring phase, management defined five critical business initiatives (CBIs), including a financial one with three components: to return the company to the breakeven point, to improve gross margins, and to improve the RONA. Management accepted that it would be difficult to improve margins and cash flow and to grow at the same time, so it set improvement in margins and RONA as the first priorities. To improve RONA, the company began a process that would reduce manufacturing costs and increase utilization of manufacturing plants. During phase one, the company reduced its number of manufacturing plants from 14 to 8.

Selection of CFROI Model

In 1992, the company introduced two incentive plans, one that compensated its top 400 executives based on RONA, and one that compensated senior executives based on ROE and growth in equity. While implementing the ROE-based incentive plan, Amelio accepted that there was not a very high correlation between ROE and share price. He and Macleod sought an alternative approach that had, as a key element, a significantly better correlation between operating behavior and share price.

Investors and analysts judged National Semiconductor's performance by accounting-based measures such as ROE, ROA, and EPS. Internally, the company was more driven by various revenue, operating, and expense metrics that rolled up into profit before taxes and RONA. The CFROI model appeared to link internal and external perceptions. The company looked at a consulting firm's correlation analyses that compared how well several metrics explained shareholder value creation in the S&P 500 companies. It agreed with a perception that there was a poor correlation between earnings growth rates and price-earnings ratios, a somewhat better correlation between RONA and price-book multiples, and a reasonably good correlation between CFROI and the ratio of market value to investment as defined by the model. National Semiconductor was moving toward a RONA focus and already had addressed the issues relating to the development of balance sheets for each of its businesses—a big move for an organization that had been highly centralized with manufacturing facilities shared among business units. The CFROI metric was similar in some ways to RONA, but it included a number of detailed adjustments relating to depreciation, inflation, and leases. The improved correlation suggested that this metric was a logical next step.

Rationale of Cash Flow Return on Investment

The proponents of the CFROI model believe that traditional accounting-based metrics have a number of weaknesses. For example, they point out that EPS is not cash based. It does not incorporate the company's asset base and does not take inflation into account. Economic-value-added and RONA measures focus on depreciating book investment, not original cash investment. Returns on depreciated assets are often unrealistically high and serve as a disincentive to invest in new assets. Economic-value-added measures are not inflation adjusted, and they do not include any assumptions on continuing investment in the business or fading performance.

Proponents of CFROI see a number of weaknesses in traditional discounted cash-flow valuation methods. Projected cash flows are only estimates. Estimates of terminal value based on perpetuity calculations are equally uncertain. In their opinion, perpetuity calculations are inconsistent with empirical life-cycle evidence. Discount rates are based on past risk premiums that may not be valid currently. *Beta* is based on price volatility but does not take credit quality into account; as a result, highly creditworthy firms sometimes have relatively high *betas* and comparable firms at or near bankruptcy sometimes have relatively low *betas*. There has been little empirical testing of the accuracy of these traditional discounted cash-flow valuation methods across a broad spectrum of companies over a significant number of years.

The CFROI model attempts to remedy these deficiencies by adjusting assets for constant dollar cost, assuming that above-average returns will fade over time to market norms, assuming sustainable reinvestment in the business, and calculating a market-derived discount rate. The CFROI valuation framework has three component calculations: CFROI, spot value, and TSR.

CFROI

CFROI is a measure of current performance. It represents the average return from the business's existing projects at a particular moment. It does not take into account changes in the level of cash flow in future periods. As a measure of average performance across all existing businesses, it provides investors with an indication of the likely return on new investments that the business is expected to achieve as it maintains or increases its asset base. It assumes today's performance is normal and assesses that performance in a way that reflects the underlying return on existing investments. It assumes that the majority of projects follow a pattern close to an annuity in constant dollars. An example of this pattern is an automobile. The performance of an automobile is relatively constant during the first four or five years of its life, but toward the end of its useful life, maintenance and repair expenses tend to rise and eventually the car is replaced. This pattern is more representative of most corporate investment projects than straight-line depreciation. The economic performance of an automobile, a machine tool, or a computer with a five-year useful life does not decline by 20 percent per year; it stays relatively constant until the time it is replaced. By calculating a gross investment amount in current dollars, CFROI avoids the old-plant-new-plant trap. When assets in old plants are heavily depreciated, traditional ratios such as ROI, ROA, and RONA become artificially high relative to the known IRR at the project's inception. As a result, these ratios become artificially low when a new plant and equipment are purchased at current prices. Consequently, these ratios sometimes act as disincentives for investment in a new plant and equipment that could increase the company's efficiency and competitiveness. In contrast, CFROI goes up when companies make capital investments and improve their efficiency.

CFROI is a direct analog to internal rate of return. CFROI is the internal rate that equates the current dollar gross investment to future cash flows and the eventual release of nondepreciating assets. CFROI is a real measure, net of inflation, so it should be compared with a real cost of capital.

Figure 14-1 illustrates how a cash-on-cash measure is translated into economic performance. The $100 descending arrow represents the current dollar gross investment. The $18 ascending arrows are current dollar gross cash flows, which last for the assumed 15-year economic life of the assets. The $25 nondepreciating assets—land and working capital—are released at the end of the period. These cash flows yield a 16.62 percent IRR, or CFROI.

Simplified Measure of CFROI

There is a simplified CFROI metric that does not require an IRR calculation. This measure, variously called sustainable CFROI (SCFROI), cash return, or algebraic CFROI, is very close to the IRR calculation in many circumstances.

SCFROI is calculated by dividing operating income by gross assets, as shown in Figure 14-2. The calculation makes three adjustments that

FIGURE 14-1 CFROI

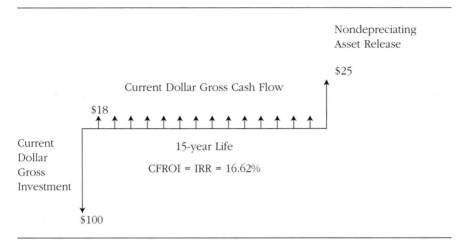

are not made for RONA: a replacement of book depreciation with economic depreciation, a capitalization of operating leases, and an inflation adjustment for capital assets. Operating income and gross assets are calculated as follows: Operating income starts with profit before taxes.

FIGURE 14-2 Calculation of SCFROI

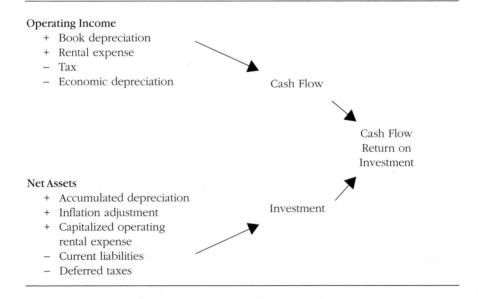

Book depreciation and amortization are added back because they are not cash expenses. Book taxes payable are subtracted, also to reflect after-tax cash flow. Rental expense is added back to eliminate any financing bias, thus assuming the company owns all the assets it actually leases. Economic depreciation, based on an estimate of the true economic life of the capital assets employed, is subtracted. The net asset calculation starts with book net assets. Accumulated depreciation is added back, nonmonetary assets are adjusted for inflation, capitalized operating rental expense is added, and current liabilities and deferred taxes are subtracted.

Because technology changes so fast in the capital-intensive semiconductor industry, accumulated depreciation is a large number for National Semiconductor. Adding back accumulated depreciation helped the company compare the performance of older businesses—which had high RONA ratios because of heavily depreciated assets—with newer, asset-intensive businesses that looked less attractive financially when evaluated by RONA.

CFROI Valuation Method

The valuation model starts with the calculation of current performance—CFROI. Then an important assumption is made based on empirical data. If a company has a high-return business, it is unlikely to maintain that return indefinitely. Experience shows that the vast majority of companies do not achieve substantial above-average performance over time. There are exceptions, but the stock market is generally not willing to pay for them. Therefore, CFROI valuation assumes that above-average returns will gradually fade to market averages. Starting with a level of cash flow based on current performance, the CFROI model calculates cash flows in future years based on an assumed fade rate and an assumed rate at which the business reinvests, constantly increasing the amount of its gross investment. The rate of increase in gross investment, or sustainable asset growth rate, is an indication of how rapidly the business can grow. In simplified form, it is calculated as follows:

Sustainable asset growth rate = $\dfrac{\text{gross cash flow minus dividends minus interest minus replacement investments}}{\text{gross investment}}$

In the CFROI spot valuation model, the accounting statement is translated into gross cash flows and gross cash investment in constant dollars to produce a cash-on-cash return. The resulting cash-on-cash return is translated to an economic performance measure by adjusting for an estimated asset life and asset mix. Then CFROI is combined with a sustainable asset growth rate and an assumed fade rate to produce a set of cash flows, which are then discounted at a market-derived rate. When this is done, a terminal valuation with a method such as a perpetuity calculation is not necessary.

The market-derived aggregate discount rate is based on a calculation that equates the present value of future cash flows produced from empirically stable asset growth rates and CFROIs with market prices for all the S&P 500 industrials. Future cash flows are calculated based on CFROI and the growth rate for the aggregate of all companies in the S&P 500 index; and then, based on the current market price of debt and equity, the discount rate is calculated. From this standard—aggregate discount rate—risk differentials for leverage and certain regulated industries are derived.

The calculation of future cash flows based on assumed fade rates and sustainable growth rates is illustrated in Table 14-1. The calculation uses the 16.62 percent IRR from Figure 14-1, with an annual cash flow of $18. The gross investment starts at $100 and increases at a rate that starts at 10 percent each year and then fades at 10 percent per year to the national average growth rate of 1.8 percent. The growth fade amount is 0.8 percent, or 10 percent of the difference between 10 and 1.8 percent. The national average IRR is 6.20, and we assume that this company's CFROI will fade toward the national average by 10 percent each year. The CFROI fade amount is 1.04 percent, or 10 percent of the difference between 16.62 and 6.20. From that fade rate, we calculate a new IRR of 15.58 and a cash flow of $18.65 for the second year. Following the same procedure for the third year, we calculate an IRR of 14.64 percent and cash flow of $19.27.

TABLE 14-1 Calculation of Future Cash Flows *(based on assumed fade rates and sustainable growth rates)*

HP-12C Calculations	This Year	One Year From Now	Two Years From Now....40 years
PV (gross investment)	-100	-110	-121
FV (nondepreciating assets)	25	27.3	29.6
n (asset life)	15	15	15
i (CFROI)	16.62%	15.58%	14.64%
PMT (gross cash flow)	18	18.65	19.27
Current IRR	16.62%	15.58%	
National Average IRR	6.20%	6.20%	
	10.42%	9.38%	
CFROI fade rate	10.00%	10.00%	
CFROI fade amount	1.04%	.94%	
Current IRR (CFROI)	16.62%	15.58%	
CFROI fade amount	(1.04%)	(.94%)	
Next year's IRR	15.58%	14.64%	
Current asset growth			
Rate for sustainable growth	10.00%	9.2%	
National average growth	1.8%	1.8%	
Difference	8.2%	7.4%	
Fade rate	10.00%	10.00%	
Growth fade amount	(.80%)	(.70%)	
Next year's growth rate	9.20%	8.50%	
This year's gross investment	100	109.2	
Next year's gross investment	109.2	118.5	
Gross cash flow		18.65	19.27
Capital commitments for growth		(9.20)	(9.30)
Capital expenditures for replacement (75/15)		(5.00)	(5.46)
Net cash flow		4.45	4.51

Total Shareholder Return

According to the CFROI model, the three factors that drive **relative total shareholder return** (TSR) are profitability, growth, and free cash flow (see Figure 14-3). Profitability, as measured by CFROI, is defined as the ability to maintain or increase earnings from the existing asset base. Growth is the ability to invest cash at rates above the cost of capital—to grow assets profitably. Free cash flow is the discipline to harvest cash and return it to shareholders when appropriate. Free cash flow, the third factor, is not currently an issue for National Semiconductor at the corporate level because it pays no dividends. It can be considered an issue at the divisional level to the extent that a division returns cash to the company. Profitability and growth together drive capital appreciation. There are trade-offs between profitability and growth, and also between growth and free cash flow. For National Semiconductor, viewing the drivers of total shareholder return in this way underscores the importance of growing as well as improving rates of return. What builds shareholder value is not just returns above the cost of capital, but the number of dollars earned above the cost of capital. A division with projects earning 3 percent more than the cost of capital can build TSR more quickly than another division of the same size with returns 5 percent above the cost of capital but a lower gross investment growth rate.

FIGURE 14-3 Three Factors Driving Total Shareholder Return

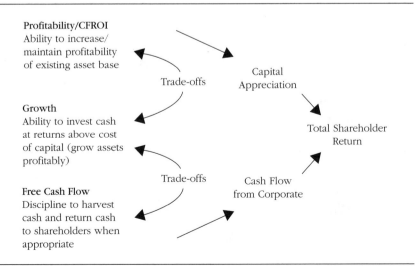

Implementing the Model

Rick Crowley, Vice President and Corporate Controller, has had primary responsibility for tailoring the model to National Semiconductor's needs and implementing it. He says that the company's biggest implementation problem has been explaining the model to operating managers. NSVM's high correlation with shareholder value comes with high complexity. Financial concepts such as the real cost of capital, the growth rate, and the fade rate of existing projects are a challenge for finance professionals as well as for those who work in different disciplines. At this point, the managers of the company's eight divisions and their four- or five-person management teams have learned how to use the model for making long-term strategic choices. For each of those strategies, they identify more traditional operating performance metrics that serve as value drivers and define day-to-day objectives for their divisions.

Training Managers to Understand NSVM

National Semiconductor's experience with adopting NSVM taught the firm that consultants skilled in implementing such a model are not always skilled in training people at all levels to use it. The finance function developed a training manual to explain the model to operating managers and walk them through the calculations. An exercise to test their understanding used published figures and the CFROI model to calculate share prices for National Semiconductor and a well-known industry competitor. This comparison was an important one for them to see, because National Semiconductor's return on net assets and profit before taxes were comparable to the competitor's, but National Semiconductor's CFROI was in the teens and the competitor's was in the high twenties.

Economic Value Discovery

The CFROI model has been a catalyst for an economic value discovery process in which National Semiconductor has compared the potential of all its businesses to build shareholder value. The NSVM valuation framework has provided a level playing field allowing each of the company's divisions to be compared using its CFROI, regardless of the capital intensity or product maturity of its business.

Corporate Portfolio Analysis

To compare the returns and growth of its portfolio of businesses, the company developed a matrix with NSVMROI on the X axis and current dollar gross investment on the Y axis. Sizes of the circles in the diagram are proportional to the amount of investment on the X axis, making businesses with larger investments stand out clearly. The 1993–95 portfolio matrix, illustrated in Figure 14-4, shows (1) two businesses that were required by corporate directive to focus on first improving their return before growing and (2) two businesses with returns above the cost of capital that increased their investment to grow. The 1995–2000 portfolio matrix, illustrated in Figure 14-5, shows the potential return targets and planned investments for four businesses, all earning more than the cost of capital and continuing to improve their returns. Business #8 has the highest return and is making the largest investment to grow.

FIGURE 14-4 1993–1995 Portfolio Matrix *(based on hypothetical numbers)*

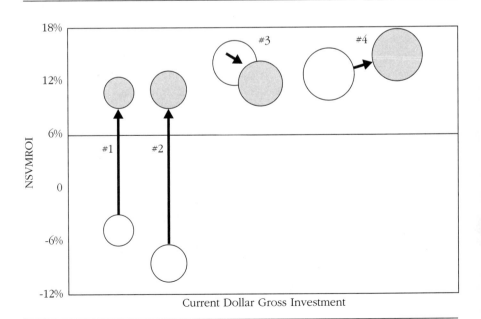

FIGURE 14-5 1995–2000 Portfolio Matrix *(based on hypothetical numbers)*

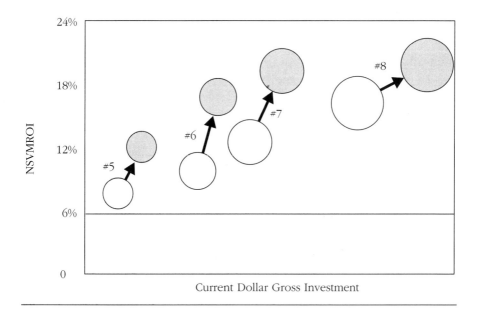

Identifying Value Drivers

National Semiconductor's Data Management Division provides an example of how value drivers were identified. In an effort coordinated by Chris Phillips, Director of Finance, the division's management team determined from their NSVM value discovery process that most of the leverage in the value computation comes from an increase in cash generation and an increase in the book value of the business. They identified the principal value drivers in both of those categories. The division was in a commodity business, with relatively mature plants and declining profit margins on mature products. It was historically a cash cow. Management required the division to continue throwing out cash for the rest of the organization, while minimizing its cash investment. To generate more cash, the division needed (1) to increase the return from its R&D investment, moving away from mature commodity products with lower profit margins and toward newer products with higher margins; (2) to reduce manufacturing costs; and (3) to refresh its capital base. Other objectives defined by the management team included reducing inventory by limiting the number of products offered and improving order-to-delivery cycles, identifying when manufacturing in-house yields better returns and when it is more economical to subcontract to other manufacturers, increasing labor productivity, and value-engineering material costs.

The CFROI measure helped the division justify investing in new plant and equipment. The old RONA measure had benefited the division by showing relatively high returns on depreciated assets, but also had supported the conventional wisdom of forgoing investments in new plant and equipment.

Rather than modeling based on revenue, gross operating profit, and profit before taxes, the division took the CFROI model all the way through to the balance sheet, and to the division's impact on TSR and overall company share price. The model showed that a small deterioration in product pricing for one of the division's commodity products had a large negative impact on the company's share price.

Ranking Investments

NSVM has been used to compare and rank both product divisions and manufacturing facilities. One high-technology product division that looked promising found in its value discovery analysis that slower-than-expected market adoption of its products had a negative impact on its value creation. It has since merged with another division.

A group of investment measures ranging from simple payback to CFROI have been used to compare and rank the company's investments in manufacturing facilities throughout the world. For each manufacturing location, the company has calculated the cumulative cash flow over 10 years; the cumulative discounted cash flow over the same period; the 10-year total shareholder return (as a percent) using the CFROI model; and the unit cost of manufacturing a wafer at the end of the period. The rankings according to TSR and discounted cash flow are close but not exactly the same.

Setting a Corporate Value Target

As a prologue to its strategic planning process, and to focus the divisions on the creation of shareholder value, the company set a specific goal for market capitalization and annual TSR to be achieved by 1999.

The TSR benchmark was determined by looking at average returns for the S&P 400 and the Value Line Semiconductor Index for five-year periods starting each year from 1960 to 1992.

Management then challenged all the divisions to come up with plans to support the company's overall TSR growth goal. Based on the strategic plan and the NSVM model, the company computed a spot value for each division. It divided the total of all spot values by the number of shares outstanding to derive the contribution each division made to the company's share price. It used a bar chart to show which divisions were not achieving and which were surpassing the company goal. Each division could then see what portion of the improving stock price it was responsible for achieving during the plan period.

Peer Comparison

As National Semiconductor moved from its restructuring phase to its growth phase, it realized that its business strategies and investment decision making would have to change. Management did a peer comparison with several other high-technology companies to identify the trade-offs they had made as they moved from normal- to high-growth phases. It selected a personal computer manufacturer, a significant player in the semiconductor business, and two other large multinational electronics companies. It compared sales growth rates, cash-flow returns, and TSRs for those companies over five-year periods. One started from a large asset base, grew both assets and revenues, and registered an annual TSR of more than 30 percent for the period. Another increased its TSR sharply by dropping its margins. The third was forced to slash its gross margins but maintained a good TSR because of a very high sales growth rate. The fourth was able to combine high profit margins with growth to achieve a compounded TSR of more than 30 percent for the period; its accounting returns were lower than National Semiconductor's, but it was growing faster. The peer group comparison provided management with a range of strategic choices as the company moved into its growth phase. Combined with the NSVM value discovery process, the comparison helped management reach a consensus to invest more aggressively in R&D and manufacturing facilities to support continued growth.

Incentive Compensation

National Semiconductor has developed a performance award plan for executives based on ROE and a cumulative annual revenue growth rate (CAGR) as a proxy for asset growth (see Figure 14-6). A matrix compares ROE on the X axis and CAGR on the Y axis. TSR equivalency lines, which the company calls "ISO-TSR" lines, are drawn on the matrix to represent levels of total shareholder return and corresponding levels of executive bonuses.[1] Each TSR equivalency line represents combinations of ROE and CAGR that are required for a given percentage of TSR. For example, the line representing X TSR, and a 100 percent payout for executives, is indifferent to a combination of 20 percent ROE and 10 percent CAGR, or 15 percent ROE and 15 percent CAGR.

FIGURE 14-6 Growth Incentive Plan*

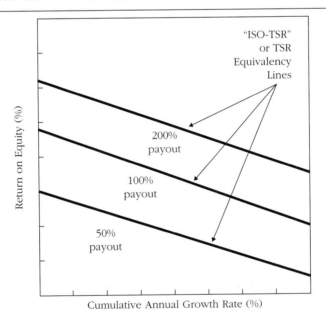

*Numbers not provided to ensure confidentiality.

[1] The prefix "ISO" in the term "ISO-TSR" line comes from the Greek word *isochronous*, meaning characterized by or occurring at equal intervals of time. The word is frequently used by electrical engineers. For example, the voice, data, and video signals in a telephone video conference call are isochronous.

RONA had been the key measure of executive performance during the restructuring phase. As the company moved into its growth phase, it needed new measures. RONA tends to act as an investment disincentive, showing high returns on depreciated assets and low returns on new assets purchased at current prices. When the CFROI is measured using NSVM, these distortions are eliminated. The NSVM model provided the basis for the new incentive system, which encourages managers to invest in order to grow and to make phase two a reality. Growing a business might cause a drop in profitability and RONA, but can still increase the value of the company as long as returns are above the cost of capital. The NSVM and the "ISO-TSR" equivalency lines on the matrix helped executives understand how sacrificing their rates of return and growing faster could increase shareholder value.

How the Value Management Model Is Used

The calculations for National Semiconductor's NSVM model are illustrated step by step in Table 14-2. The model is consistent with the CFROI methodology, but adapted to the company's needs. The value of the company is the sum of two components—capitalized income and the current value of depreciating and nondepreciating assets.

Income is first adjusted to replace book depreciation with economic depreciation, to capitalize lease expenses, and to charge for the effects of inflation. Economic depreciation is based on current dollar value, average age, and estimated life of capital assets. The inflation charge covers the loss of purchasing power because cash is tied up in nonmonetary assets.

The resulting NSVM gross income is charged with a real cost of capital. Then NSVM gross income is capitalized with a perpetuity formula that reflects both the estimated rate of growth in gross investment and the estimated fade rate. The result is NSVM net income valuation.

The current dollar net investment is the sum of the value of nondepreciating assets, the current dollar value of depreciating assets, and capitalized rental expenses, with an adjustment for the age of depreciating assets. The value of the company is the sum of NSVM net income valuation and the current dollar net investment.

TSR is the IRR of the plan. It assumes that the plan is a project in which the initial investment is today's spot value, cash is generated each year, and the ending spot value is the value of the business at the end of the project. This logic is the same as that illustrated for CFROI in Figure 14-1.

TABLE 14-2 National Semiconductor Value Management Model

Calculation	Explanation
NSVM Current Profit	
1. Profit before taxes	Book profit before taxes
2. Plus book depreciation and amortization	Add back noncash expenses
3. Minus book taxes payable	To reflect after-tax cash flow
4. Plus rental expense	Assume the company owns the asset to eliminate financing bias
5. Equals NSVM current profit	Result is cash generated by the business before investment decisions
NSVM Gross Income	
6. NSVM current profit (per item 5)	
7. Minus inflation charge	Loss of purchasing power because cash is tied up in nonmonetary assets
8. Minus real depreciation charge	Annual payment to replace assets as they wear out
	Formula: $\dfrac{(c\,A)}{(1+c)^{L-1}}$
	where
	c = real cost of capital
	A = current dollar value of gross depreciating assets
	L = estimated life of assets
9. Equals NSVM gross income	Amount of cash left after maintaining asset base
	Numerator used for deriving NSVMROI
NSVM Income Valuation	
10. NSVM gross income (per item 9)	

TABLE 14-2 (continued)

Calculation	Explanation
11. Minus capital utilization charge	An adjustment to show the return relative to the cost of capital because investors expect their money to generate a return higher than the cost of capital before any value is created
	Nominal cost of capital = inflation rate times cost of capital
	Formulas:
	Real cost of capital times gross investment (excluding capitalized rental)
	Nominal cost of capital times capitalized rental
12. Equals NSVM net income	Cash generated above cost of capital
13. Times capitalization factor	Converts NSVM net income into perpetuity value
	Formula: $\dfrac{1}{c + f - g}$
	where
	c = real cost of capital f = fade rate g = real growth in gross investment
14. Equals NSVM net income valuation	Item 12 times item 13

NSVM Asset Valuation

15. Nondepreciating assets	
16. Plus current dollar value of gross depreciating assets	Brings existing depreciating assets value to current value as a result of inflation
17. Plus capitalized rental expense	Assume rental expense is being capitalized at nominal cost of capital (of less concern to a company without substantial leased assets)
18. Equals current dollar gross investment	
19. Minus age adjustment	Percentage of depreciating assets value that has been used up
20. Equals current dollar net investment	Current dollar gross investment minus age adjustment

TABLE 14-2 (continued)

Calculation	Explanation
NSVM Spot Value	
21. Sum of net income valuation (line 14) and current dollar net investment (line 20)	Total unadjusted value as seen by potential investor at any point in time
NSVMROI (%)	
22. NSVM gross income (line 9) divided by average current dollar gross investment (line 18)	Rate of return generated from shareholders' investment at present value—represents relative value-creating ability of the business
	Formula:
	$$\frac{\text{NSVM Gross Income}}{\text{Adjusted NSVM Current \$ Gross Investment}}$$
23. TSR (%)	The rate of return that equates today's spot value, the initial investment, with cash flows generated in future years and a spot value for the business at the end of the period

People Interviewed

Richard D. Crowley, Jr., Vice President and Corporate Controller
Donald Macleod, Executive Vice President and Chief Financial Officer
Christine Phillips, Director of Finance, Data Management Division

15

PepsiCo, Inc.

Growth always has been an overriding goal for PepsiCo. Chairman and CEO Wayne Calloway says, "If we're not a growth company, we're nothing." Indeed the company has a record to be proud of—with compounded annual growth rates over the past decade of 15 percent in sales, 24 percent in net income, 24 percent in earnings per share, and 14 percent in net cash provided by continuing operations. PepsiCo's objective going forward is balanced growth—a balance among earnings growth, capital spending growth, and cash-flow growth. Managers throughout the company have been accustomed to thinking in terms of earnings growth; now they also are being challenged to think about cash-flow and return-on-capital growth as well.

Financial Metrics

In its annual report, PepsiCo describes these four metrics: volume growth, operating profit growth, cash growth, and investment returns above the company's estimated 11 percent WACC.

Volume Growth

Volume growth is important for two reasons. First, the company always tries to leverage its sales by growing profits faster than revenues, but it can only increase profits so much by cutting costs and improving productivity. Second, volume or unit growth is the long-term driver of growth in shareholder value.

Treasurer Randy Barnes believes that some companies are so focused on return on sales and productivity that they don't think enough

159

about the top line. They become more and more productive by eliminating their growth resources. Calloway likes to see marketing leverage, or continued reinvestment to build market share and revenues. For example, Frito-Lay will grow 12 percent in both sales and earnings this year, yet people wonder why it cannot leverage its sales growth more in such a consumer business. The company has consciously decided to reinvest through pricing below inflation and to build its market share at this time, because it believes its competition is in disarray. The competition wonders why PepsiCo is not insisting on higher margins. The reason is that Frito-Lay's market share is growing by three to four percentage points each year.

Cash Growth

Cash growth is a requirement for PepsiCo's core strategy of continually reinvesting free cash flow to grow, particularly overseas.

Operating Profit Growth

Maintaining profit margins is a particular challenge when PepsiCo is expanding into new markets overseas and using value pricing to maintain or enhance market share. Innovative ideas are required to reduce costs. For example, the company has improved Taco Bell's operating margins by having suppliers prepare ingredients so that they can be assembled in the restaurant. This move has reduced space requirements for the kitchen at individual Taco Bell outlets by 50 percent.

Despite the increasing importance placed on cash flow, PepsiCo still believes it must meet its objectives and deliver consistent growth in quarterly EPS. Archcompetitor Coca-Cola sets an example by being very consistent. If PepsiCo's quarterly EPS growth starts to dip below its historic rates, analysts can be expected to reduce their long-term growth estimates accordingly.

Investment Returns

To produce investment returns well above the company's estimated 11 percent WACC, PepsiCo has defined hurdle rates of 14 percent in developed countries, 16 percent in "almost developed" countries, and 18 percent in developing countries. The company adjusts its hurdle rates as a proxy for a more full-blown probability analysis with risk-adjusted cash flows. It sets a minimum 14 percent hurdle rate because it does not want to encourage projects that are just marginally above the cost of capital.

Barnes cites the following example to reinforce the need for returns above the cost of capital to create value: A national brewer invested $50 per barrel to gain market share and used its marketing prowess to put many other brewers out of business. The brewer invested about $2 billion and made $100 million pretax. Another smaller company bought a number of the distressed breweries for $2 to $4 per barrel. The cost of capital at the time was about 14 percent, and the smaller brewer had an 18 percent cost-of-sales return advantage. For the larger brewer, growth has actually destroyed value, and no amount of marketing expertise can compensate for insufficient investment returns.

Barnes uses the following example to help company managers understand why PepsiCo requires a 14 percent return when its cost of capital is 11 percent. An overseas manager of Pizza Hut International who is delivering $5 million profits may say that he can deliver $10 million with twice as many stores, or $20 million with four times as many. But if such an expansion requires an investment of $100 million, PepsiCo earns a return about equal to its cost of capital and creates hardly any value. Barnes asks, "Do you want to spend 10 years of your life just earning the cost of capital and adding no value? We can repurchase $1 billion of PepsiCo shares per year with one person spending an hour a day and create more shareholder value."

PepsiCo also has to adjust its thinking on international investments to fit local conditions. It has a franchisee in Brazil whose rule of thumb is to invest only when he expects to get back all his money in three years, which implies a return of more than 25 percent. Therefore, PepsiCo does not want people developing 20-year models for Brazil, because nobody is smart enough to know what will happen in 20 years. This country needs a shorter-term horizon. If the returns are not at least 18 to 20 percent in such an economic environment, it is better to stop investing because the company is not making money.

Holistic Approach to Performance Measures

PepsiCo uses a full range of traditional financial performance measures. Mary Jo Shotting, Director, Corporate Development, says, "This company tries to take a holistic approach to the different measures, not just focusing on one or two. However, some measures get more emphasis because of their contribution to value. You'd be hard-pressed to talk to any of our division CFOs and not hear what his or her return on capital was."

PepsiCo has analyzed other measurement systems such as economic value added and CFROI and lined them up against its own discounted cash-flow and value driver approach. Shotting points out that all of these measures are designed to help a company improve its cash flow. "If you are already focusing as many people as possible on your cash-flow value drivers," she says, "then switching to a different measurement system doesn't necessarily give you anything more."

Shotting also expresses concern about using a complex model in which someone else has the "black box." PepsiCo would never use a model its staff could not fully understand and control. It finds that some complex models do not deliver enough additional value to be worth the time required to implement them. Shotting is concerned about any measure that requires a capital charge, such as economic value added. Capital charges, in her opinion, can allow people to trade off growth to improve their returns. For example, when a manager has difficulty growing earnings (the numerator), he or she may concentrate on shrinking assets employed (the denominator), and consequently slow the growth of the business. She notes that PepsiCo's NOPAT and capital employed are actually not far from the numbers that would be used with economic value added. If the company grossed up its investment base by adding back amortized goodwill, the ROI ratios would theoretically be equalized for performance measurement purposes. Some of PepsiCo's businesses have steadily increasing ROIs because the amortization of goodwill keeps reducing their investment bases. However, management takes the reasons for those increases into account when comparing performance among all the businesses.

Shotting believes that being consistent over time is more important than the measure used. Whether or not adjustments are made to earnings and the capital base, the important thing is to get a better return on those assets from one year to the next.

Constraints on Growth

PepsiCo has a single-A credit rating and a degree of leverage it considers optimal. The company is confident of retaining this rating, because of its strong cash flow. But looking in the other direction, Barnes believes that moving up to a double-A or triple-A rating is not worth the cost. Some consumer products companies with double-A ratings have borrowing costs as much as 200 basis points higher than PepsiCo's because their debt management is so conservative. They tend to have a high portion of long-term, fixed-rate debt.

In 1988, PepsiCo bought a number of bottlers, and in the process took its leverage to record-high levels. Analysts asked Calloway when the company was going to reduce its debt. He said never, because debt has a 4 percent after-tax cost, and the company can either invest at or above its 14 percent hurdle rate or buy back stock for a return of 13 percent.

In recent years, buying back stock has been a good way for PepsiCo to deliver returns to its stockholders in the form of capital gains. However, management keeps the limitations of this approach in mind. Beyond a certain point, buying back stock can be dangerous for a company that wants to grow because it reduces the amount the company can borrow and can play havoc with some accounting-based ratios. CFO Bob Dettmer did a study a few years ago showing that if the company bought back 17 percent of its shares, its book equity would be wiped out. Buying back shares increases ROE but also increases the debt-to-book-equity ratio. If the company is selling at a multiple of book value, every share the company buys back in effect takes the equivalent of five shares from its book capitalization. This result shows how misleading some accounting-based measures can be. PepsiCo cannot completely ignore them, but it emphasizes coverage ratios more than debt-to-book-equity ratios.

Capital Spending Parameters

Historically, capital has not been a constraint and has not held back PepsiCo's growth in any way. As long as new opportunities have met the company's return standards, they have generally been approved.

When Calloway became chairman, he pushed everybody hard for earnings growth and sales growth, and for four or five years that growth was delivered. During that time, Barnes considered trying to establish some return-on-capital targets, but returns were far above the cost of capital, and he was concerned that such targets might inhibit the company's growth. Then for several years, growth in capital spending exceeded PepsiCo's growth in sales and profits—the company was investing too much capital for the earnings growth it was achieving. Now the firm is putting particular emphasis on cash-flow growth as it reviews and approves new projects. Barnes believes that PepsiCo still should be a growth company but needs to grow through innovation and ideas, not just through the brute force of capital investments.

A change in mentality is required. A beverage person might say, "I know if I put out another vending machine, it's a good decision. It helps me sell more, increase market share, and deliver more profit." But Barnes would tell him that the move also has to help the company by earning a positive return above the cost of capital. Even when people understand what ROI and hurdle rates are, additional efforts are needed to ensure that investments earn returns above the cost of capital. Good business people are by definition optimistic. They know that by continuing to invest they will grow their market share and earnings, and they hope for adequate investment returns as well. But actual returns above the cost of capital are what drive share price growth.

For example, the company's beverage business recently found that its inventory of vending machines being refurbished was large enough to satisfy every customer need for a few months and thus save the business from buying new machines. If capital is free, marketing managers will prefer to buy a new machine rather than to repair an old one. A new machine looks better—it has more capacity and more features such as coin changers, and it has lower operating costs—but you might not be able to get the required return. A new machine costs $1,500 in capital, and refurbishing costs only $150.

On the other hand, the company is switching many of its convenience store sales from 12-ounce cans and 16-ounce bottles to 20- and 32-ounce bottles. Rather than selling a 12-ounce can for 65 cents, the stores will sell a 32-ounce bottle for 99 cents. By trading the customer up to the 99-cent bottle, PepsiCo and its retail customers collect 34 cents more and everybody in the chain makes money, while the customer gets almost three times as much Pepsi. A capital investment is required, and of course it must meet the return, but Barnes's point is that this project is idea driven; it does not just throw out more money to do the same things the company always has been doing.

Developing a Cash-Flow Mentality

Bob Carleton, Senior Vice President and Controller, believes that companies like PepsiCo must orient themselves toward generating cash over the longer term but also be aware that Wall Street still looks at earnings. Even leading proponents of discounted cash-flow valuation agree with the Statement of Financial Accounting Concepts—that earnings under the accrual system for the current year are the best predictor of future cash flow.

Carleton points out that common standards have not yet been as well developed for cash-flow measurements as they have for accrual accounting measurements. For example, there is not a universally understood definition of free cash flow.

Managers at PepsiCo have learned over the years how to manage for revenue and earnings growth but have not yet learned quite as well how to manage for cash-flow growth. At this point, some see it as an additional burden.

Some people will complain that cash-flow growth cannot be as high as earnings growth when investing for returns several years from now, but Barnes believes that for PepsiCo in total, it is reasonable to manage so that cash flow and earnings grow at about the same rate. The international side is different. Those businesses often require net investments with negative cash flow for a number of years while they are developing their markets.

The focus on cash flows makes people think in new ways. For example, the company is starting to refranchise its restaurants—selling them to franchisees—and believes that this move could pull more than $500 million out of the restaurant business without changing earnings at all.

One of PepsiCo's restaurant divisions is in the process of "reconcepting" and, with the success of this process, plans to add a number of new units. Historically, new capital has been required for new units. But PepsiCo has challenged the division to generate cash for the new units by refranchising existing units. That way the division gets a double win; it redeploys money from lower-return assets to higher-return assets.

Barnes emphasizes that PepsiCo still has enough capital for virtually any investment it wants to make. "The key is to discipline ourselves to make sure we make only the investments that deliver the returns we promise and not kid ourselves with overly optimistic projections of profit growth and returns to justify poor or overpriced investments," he says.

Adjusting Metrics for Emerging Markets

PepsiCo is investing in many developing countries where competitors like Coca-Cola are not yet entrenched. The opportunities for investment are huge, but one of the biggest constraints is finding people capable of capitalizing on them. Besides worrying about returns above its hurdle rates, PepsiCo also must consider investments in developing markets that should be made today, while there is still an opportunity to become established, but will not pay off for years. Capital budgeting in emerging markets is almost an oxymoron. Different rules of thumb are required. The sales productivity metrics and maximum acceptable amount to invest per case must be adapted to local market conditions.

Barnes says, "We believe in our businesses." The company might be in many emerging markets for as long as five to eight years before seeing much of a profit. For example, developing the China market might require a $500 million investment, and after running its models the company might not be confident that the investment returns will exceed its hurdle rates. But Barnes asks, "Are we going to just cede the business to Coke because we weren't willing to take the risk on a $500 million investment?"

The faster the growth a market offers, the more difficult it is to earn a return because everybody jumps in at the same time. Barnes cites the example of cellular telephones. Everyone was losing money when there were 16 competitors, all cutting prices and adding features. No one was going to make any money until the market sorted down to four or five players. A company had to decide if it had the wherewithal to stick it out and be one of the survivors.

PepsiCo's experience in emerging markets gives it an idea of what kind of productivity to expect. For example, using rough numbers, sales productivity for route deliveries in a country in Eastern Europe might be 70 percent of what it is in more developed markets, and vending machine throughput might be 50 percent. The company has to decide how fast it wants to grow. It does not want to over-invest while it is still training people and bringing its productivity up to international standards. But if it does not grow fast enough, it will find that Coke added routes twice as fast and has five times its market share; and even though Pepsi has brought productivity up to international standards, it is lagging in market share.

How the Company Values Itself

PepsiCo projects cash flows based on current strategies for each of its businesses. It values each business and then values the enterprise as a whole, comparing that value with PepsiCo's current market value. Chuck Darville, Manager, Corporate Strategic Planning, points out that most of this evaluation is prospective. Not much time is spent analyzing past strategies and performance and how they have been valued by the market.

The strategic planning staff calculates valuations based on known strategies, including expansion plans, required investment and projected cash flow from new products, and capital required to sustain current operations. If there is a substantial difference between the internal valuation and the market's valuation, they try to understand the reason. The market may not have enough information, it may not fully understand the company strategy, or it may just be valuing the company strategy differently.

Valuations are based on long-term strategies. The duration of the company's long-term planning horizon is 12 years. At the end of that period, it calculates a no-growth perpetuity, assuming returns for additional dollars invested will not exceed the cost of capital. Planning is most detailed for the first three years. Though the 12-year forecast is far more detailed than a trend line, projected returns tend to move toward the cost of capital in the later years.

The company has not changed its 12-year duration in recent years, but it continually checks the implied durations of comparable companies in each of the three business sectors. For PepsiCo and the other comparable companies, an investment information service publishes stock price forecasts and assumptions on value drivers such as sales growth, operating profit margin, capital expenditures as a percentage of sales, working capital, the cash tax rate, and the weighted average cost of capital. It is possible to use those assumptions to do discounted cash-flow valuations for each of the companies. Then an investment information service's projected stock price can be used to solve for the duration—the point in time when the growth assumptions for the value drivers no longer apply and a no-growth perpetuity is used.

PepsiCo does a base valuation using known strategies that do not include any acquisitions, and then identifies other strategies that may create additional value. It may look at alternative ways to invest a given amount of cash to create additional value. The valuation is based on three-year plans submitted by business units, but those units may submit additional investment proposals not envisioned in the plan. A clear distinction is made between what is known today and incremental investments.

PepsiCo calculates a cost of capital for each of its business sectors—beverages, snack foods, and restaurants. It continually analyzes comparable companies to verify that the beta is appropriate for each sector and for the company as a whole. Currently, the company assumes a uniform 11 percent WACC for all three sectors.

Financial Reporting Systems

Business units send performance reports to headquarters every four weeks. Actual results are compared with the plan. The reports contain externally reported financial information such as revenues and profits, internal accounting information such as allocated costs, and nonfinancial information such as market share and other operating measures particular to each business. The information systems were designed primarily for accounting-based information. Adding nonfinancial information to the standard report formats is sometimes difficult.

How Investors and Analysts
Value the Company

Barnes thinks that securities analysts generally understand cash flow, but that they are focused more on earnings. Most of them are trying to earn their reputation by calling a turn in the stocks they follow, such as PepsiCo's recent rise from $47 to $58.

Barnes believes that most of PepsiCo's investors are long-term investors, but he acknowledges that there are also momentum investors who move in and out. They tend to react quickly to what people from the company say. When the stock was at $39, Calloway gave a talk about pulling back on the level of new restaurant investment and getting stricter on return criteria, and the stock went up to $42. Vice Chairman Roger Enrico further elaborated on the restaurant sector's investment plans and gave a cash-flow estimate for restaurants for the year, which brought the stock to $46. Others in the company elaborated on marketing plans for beverages and snack foods and reiterated the concern that new investments meet certain returns. That helped drive the stock to its high of $58.

PepsiCo recently talked to a number of analysts who follow the company to find out what valuation models they use. Some analysts admit that a cash-flow analysis is the right way to value a company; and some are beginning to invest in models to help them do cash-flow valuations, but they still appear to be in the minority. Most of them are concerned with price-earnings ratios when they compare the company's current and past performance to others. If a company's price-earnings ratio is currently below the industry average but has been historically above, it may be considered undervalued. Some analysts say that a cash-flow analysis is a selling tool. If they want to put a stock on the buy list, they may use a cash-flow analysis to strengthen their argument that a company is undervalued.

Many of these analysts cover 40, 60, or even 80 companies. Shotting points out that it takes the entire strategic planning department six weeks to value PepsiCo—that is 40 people valuing one company, as opposed to one analyst looking at 40 companies.

People Interviewed

Randall C. Barnes, Senior Vice President and Treasurer
Robert L. Carleton, Senior Vice President and Controller
Charles W. Darville, Manager, Corporate Strategic Planning
Mary Jo Shotting, Director, Corporate Development

16

Pioneer Hi-Bred International, Inc.

Pioneer High-Bred is the leading breeder and producer of hybrid seed corn in the world. The company was founded in 1926 to apply newly discovered genetic techniques to produce this product. Today it develops, produces, and markets hybrids of corn, sorghum, sunflower, and vegetables, and varieties of soybean, alfalfa, wheat, and canola. In North America it has a 45 percent share of the seed corn market and an 18 percent share of the soybean seed market and substantial market shares in Europe as well: About 29 percent of the company's sales and about 28 percent of its operating profits are accrued outside North America. Pioneer Hi-Bred operates on all continents, conducting research in 29 countries and selling in 100 countries.

A large part of Pioneer Hi-Bred's value is based on intellectual property. The company's ability to develop new products and remain competitive comes from continued R&D, and budgeting for R&D is an integral part of Pioneer Hi-Bred's business planning. Yet the company does not capitalize R&D expenses for internal analysis, and NPV analysis plays only a small role in its research spending decisions. In determining research priorities, the company considers a whole portfolio of opportunities and compares expected rewards with factors such as the amount of investment required, the company's technological competitive position, the probability of technical success, and the estimated time required to bring a product to the market.

Pioneer Hi-Bred's most important assets are the genetic resources, known as germplasm, developed through plant breeding and laboratory research. Competition in the seed industry is based on price, product performance, and service. The company's objective is to produce products that consistently outperform the competition and thus command a premium price, but achieving this objective requires ongoing investment in R&D of proprietary products. Continued improvement in the performance of the company's products is required to maintain profit margins and market share. R&D expenditures are normally about 7.5 percent of sales and equal to the level of capital expenditures. As one rough measure of the importance of research and other intangibles, the company's stock trades at approximately 4.5 times book value. Pioneer Hi-Bred considers protection of its proprietary products vital to its ability to support continued research and product development and generate an adequate return to shareholders. The company maintains ownership of and controls the use of inbreds and varieties in the United States through patents and the Plant Variety Protection Act of 1970. Both the patents and the Act essentially prohibit other parties from selling seed made from these inbreds and varieties until such protection expires, usually well after the useful life of the seed. Outside the United States, the level of protection varies from country to country according to local law and international agreement.

Pioneer Hi-Bred has been a public company since 1973. It sold its beef cattle and poultry operations in the late 1970s and sold a company that made portable communication devices used in the retail industry in the late 1980s. It redeployed the capital from these sales into its core seed operations. The company's business is cyclical because of factors that affect seed purchases, such as crop inventories, commodity prices, and government programs to control the number of acres planted. However, Pioneer Hi-Bred believes that when farmers have an economic incentive to plant, they will buy seed and try to limit other expenses.

Pioneer Hi-Bred's goal is to finance its growth with earnings, and the company has very low leverage. A conservative financial structure helps it endure business cycles and bear the technical risk characteristic of a research-based organization. From time to time when it considers its stock undervalued, Pioneer Hi-Bred buys back its own shares in the open market with excess cash.

Pioneer Hi-Bred's principal financial performance metrics are ROE and growth in EPS. In the late 1980s, management saw that Pioneer Hi-Bred's historic leadership position in the seed industry was beginning to slip. The firm's financial performance and share price were not up to its expectations. ROE was 11.2 percent in 1990, so management set a goal of 20 percent by 1995. ROE reached 21.2 percent after adjustment for unusual events in 1994, and the company set a continuing goal of at least 20 percent ROE and double-digit annual EPS growth.

Adoption of ROE Measure

Management adopted ROE in conjunction with a continuing focus on ROA at the business-unit level because the measure was easy to explain throughout the company, and it could be used to drive the kind of behavior that would enhance shareholder value. It has been a challenge for management to explain to people at various levels what the company's financial goals are and how each of their jobs relates to the achievement of those goals. The ROE concept has made it easier for employees to understand how the company makes decisions and how those decisions affect financial returns and shareholder value. Plant managers have learned how improving production yield and reducing inventory can increase ROE. Other groups are seeing how measures such as increased margins or market shares affect the company's ROE. Management explains that the improvement in a business unit's ROA from year to year adds to shareholder value; and Pioneer Hi-Bred can easily track this value because its financial structure stays essentially the same over time.

Nonfinancial Performance Measures

Pioneer Hi-Bred is moving toward a balanced scorecard of financial and nonfinancial performance measures for its business units. The company tracks a number of nonfinancial measures that do not directly drive compensation. They include customer satisfaction, product performance advantage, market share, and pricing in relation to value.

The finance group plays an important role in the creation of nonfinancial measures. It develops ideas, conducts analyses, makes recommendations, and works in partnership with business managers to determine whether certain measures can be effective in managing a business. Finance also helps managers set their own benchmarks.

Benchmarks are important tools for focusing people's attention and energy and getting them to think about new ways of doing things. For example, finance set five days as a target for closing the books at the end of the year—a goal that seemed unreasonable and out of reach. In order to meet the goal, the finance people acknowledged they had to change the way they closed the books, and they started to think creatively about how procedures could be improved and what kind of training and development was required.

R&D Budgeting

Managing research expenditures is a key part of Pioneer Hi-Bred's strategic planning. R&D is the very foundation for the company's current products and its future. Though research takes place all over the world, it is managed centrally through a shared decision-making process among people from the marketing, finance, and technical functions. The company balances the amount it spends on research and development every year with its principal financial goals—a minimum 20 percent ROE and double-digit annual EPS growth. Paul Matson, Director of Finance—Research and Product Development, explains that the R&D process itself defines some boundaries. Because of its long-term nature, R&D cannot be pumped up one year and cut back the next. If additional funds were allocated, there would be a limit on how much could be absorbed. If R&D spending were cut back, some ongoing programs probably would be damaged. R&D expenditures are not charged to business units because the benefits of those expenditures are spread across many units over an indefinite period. Pioneer Hi-Bred does not capitalize R&D expenditures, but in its strategic planning process these expenditures are treated as capital assets. Vice President and Treasurer Joe Dollison says, "We lean more toward simplicity in accounting for intellectual property, but we recognize that our investment decisions for R&D are becoming more complex."

Plant breeding is the foundation of the company's research organization, and now Pioneer Hi-Bred also is using biotechnology to engineer traits into its germplasm base. In plant breeding, the probability of success is a function of the number of plant crosses and the breeder's skill in recognizing a product with a package of traits that fits the market. Biotechnology can shorten the process that requires years of traditional plant breeding and enable the incorporation of traits that would not be possible through plant breeding. The shift toward biotechnology has increased the level of sophistication in the research process and, as a result, Pioneer Hi-Bred has had to acquire technology from the outside through licensing, partnerships, and strategic alliances. Consequently, research spending as a percent of sales has increased in recent years.

Geography is a competitive advantage for Pioneer Hi-Bred. The company has capitalized on its widespread international network to breed and test year-round. It takes between 90 and 110 days to grow most crops. Through the use of winter nurseries in both the northern and the southern hemispheres, Pioneer Hi-Bred gets multiple generations of breeding activity in one 12-month period.

In the past, research in a given overseas region such as Latin America or Asia was primarily for seed products to be used in that region. While local product development continues to be important, an increasing number of the company's research projects are part of coordinated worldwide efforts. Germplasm is shared across all maturity zones. Hybrids that work well in southern Indiana and parts of southern Iowa might work well in Italy. Those developed in Canada and the northern United States might work well in parts of northern Europe.

As Pioneer Hi-Bred sees increasing opportunities to invest in research and moves toward increased utilization of biotechnology, it recognizes the need to analyze and prioritize its R&D projects more rigorously. Failing to identify an opportunity or investing in a project that turns out to be a bad one can be a big mistake. But the company cannot pursue every project. It has to focus on those that have the most revenue potential and long-term strategic value.

Pioneer Hi-Bred has started a research portfolio management process to make sure the company gets the biggest benefit for dollars employed and to decide on a manageable number of projects. It is developing more formal procedures for assigning priorities and allocating research dollars. It is defining minimum requirements for written proposals while trying to preserve the collegiality of the decision-making process.

Pioneer Hi-Bred seeks a balance between quantitative analysis and qualitative and strategic considerations. People are encouraged to think hard about numbers in projections, to make them as accurate as possible, and to document their underlying assumptions in writing. However, the company recognizes that research projects are subject to a great deal of uncertainty and change, and sometimes it is difficult to make accurate financial forecasts beyond one or two years. Going forward, the company would like to further analyze probabilities related to such factors as technical feasibility, research costs, market sizes, and other critical drivers in order to calculate a range of possible outcomes rather than relying on single estimates. Because of the uncertainty and time horizons of its research projects, Pioneer Hi-Bred finds that NPV analysis has limitations. It provides useful support and makes people question their assumptions, but it does not provide final answers for business decisions.

Pioneer Hi-Bred uses matrices to examine projects based on combinations of criteria. For example, Figure 16-1 shows a comparison of the NPV of research expenditures with the net present value of expected rewards for various projects. Figure 16-2 compares the net present value of the expected dollar reward with the percentage probability of technical success. The size of the bubble for each project indicates the NPV of the research expenditure. Another matrix the company uses compares the expected reward for each project, measured in millions of dollars of NPV, with technological competitive position, rated on a scale ranging from weak to dominant. Still another compares the NPV of the expected dollar reward for each project with the estimated time (in years) to market. As with quantitative analysis, these matrices do not provide answers. But Ann Bublitz, Marketing Director and Technologies Specialist, explains that they help people structure their thinking and they facilitate discussion of research priorities among research and business people.

FIGURE 16-1 Reward and Research Investments *(based on fictional numbers)*

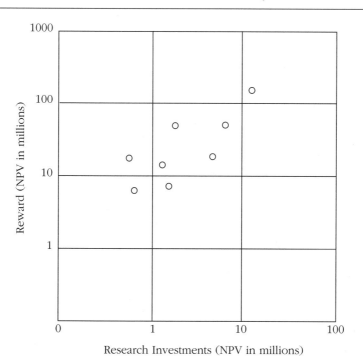

FIGURE 16-2 Reward vs. Probability of Technical Success* *(based on fictional numbers)*

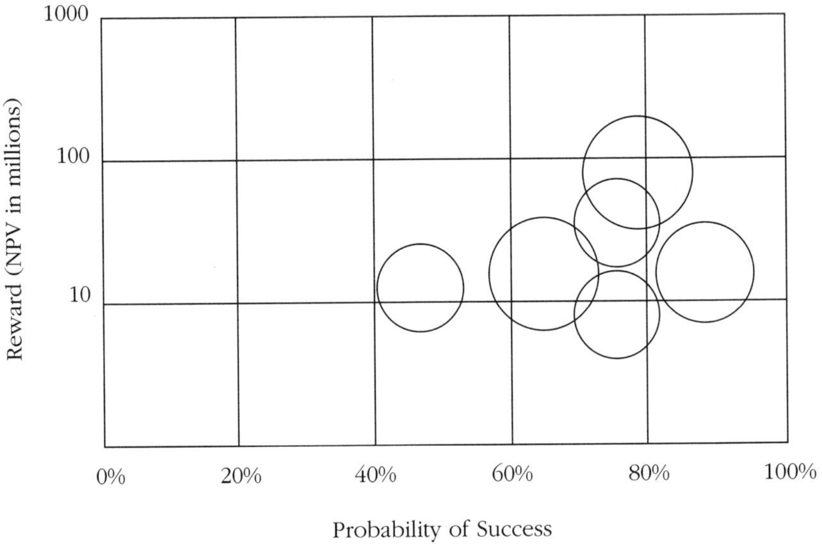

Probability of Success

* Circle size reflects research NPV.

Cooperative Decision Making

Pioneer Hi-Bred has a participative decision-making process for defining priorities in areas throughout the company including research, product development, sales, and marketing. The CEO sets a broad strategic focus and the finance group defines financial goals.

New product ideas may come from commercial business units, senior management, or product planning teams responsible for the long-range strategies for each product line. A business development function that was established in 1988 to look at new business opportunities has recently been split among marketing, research, and the planning and budgeting group in the finance function. This change was made to support the flow of ideas and plans from the business units rather than from a centralized corporate group.

Sometimes people in the company think that there are too many committees; they think decisiveness is lacking and that there is uncertainty about who is responsible for what. But Brian Hart, Vice President and Corporate Controller, believes that this cross-functional process spreads education throughout the company and builds equity in the decisions that are made. The very core of the decision-making process is the cross-functional representation from finance, marketing, sales, supply, and research management.

Pioneer Hi-Bred did a recent analysis of where it was deploying its research investment. The analysis itself did not lead to any startling conclusions, but the process was very helpful. Research scientists learned about ROI concepts and how their projects fit into the business picture.

The company also reviewed all of its R&D activities related to corn products to define priorities and identify weaknesses and opportunities. Pioneer Hi-Bred used bubble charts, such as those illustrated in Figures 16-1 and 16-2, to examine (1) the allocation of its resources among the world's most important markets and among the most important current technologies and (2) the role of the research, marketing, finance, sales, and product management functions. Though the review had a product focus, team building turned out to be a more important benefit than any specific product-related conclusions.

Cost of Capital

The company's 15 percent WACC is used as a discount rate. According to Jeff Austin, Director—Corporate Finance, Pioneer Hi-Bred has thought about setting different discount rates for projects of different risk as part of a fine-tuning process but is concerned about the difficulty of determining rates for each project. It might consider using a different discount rate for an acquisition or a project that is outside its normal sphere of activity, but it considers the calculation of a range of possible outcomes a better method for assessing risk.

Incentive Compensation

Pioneer Hi-Bred has established a compensation system based on two factors: ROE and growth in EPS. ROA serves as a proxy for ROE at the business-unit level. The level of assets is defined as receivables, inventory, and fixed assets. Except for allocating accounts among business-units, the receivables, inventory, and fixed-asset accounts are consistent with the company's published financial statements. Pioneer Hi-Bred makes virtually no adjustments to these accounts, because it believes that making a few adjustments could initiate arguments for more adjustments.

The company's reluctance to make adjustments is in line with its philosophy of simplicity, consistency, and continuity. Pioneer Hi-Bred is looking for improvement in a business unit's performance over time, accounted for on a consistent basis. This consistent improvement is more important than how assets are allocated and adjusted. The company recognizes and communicates to its managers that not every business unit can be expected to achieve the same ROA. Some will be above 40 percent; others will never get to that level. Incremental improvement is what counts, whether it be return on sales, asset utilization, or operating income growth.

The company is trying to make the new incentive measures as simple and understandable as possible. Next year, part of the reward system will be based on earnings growth and a smaller part will be based on return on equity of 20 percent or greater. There will be both current and longer-term components. Cash compensation will be based on earnings growth and ROE over a one-year period, and an award of restricted stock will be based on earnings growth measured over three years. The company is also considering an even longer-term incentive plan driven by the increase in share value over a 5- to 10-year period.

Paul Schickler, Corporate Vice President and Director of Resource Planning, cites the sales organization as an example of the way incentive compensation works at various levels. Like the CEO of the company, the vice president of sales and the sales directors are compensated based on EPS growth, both annually and over a three-year period. At the next level, sales managers responsible for a geographic area such as one or two states are compensated based on return on sales and growth in sales over time. Return on sales is calculated as contribution divided by sales. It is a measure of operating income with no allocation of interest expense. It is based on factors the sales manager can influence directly such as pricing, volume, product mix, shipping costs, fixed costs, and discounts offered in the form of seed samples. District sales managers are compensated based primarily on market share. Operating measures for plant managers include fixed-cost growth, variable cost growth, and the overall cost of production. Controllable fixed costs are mainly repairs and maintenance. Variable costs include detassling (removing tassles from seed-bearing plants to control pollination in seed fields), roguing (removing plants that can contaminate seed and impair quality), and field supervision. Plant managers also have quality measures, including the appearance of seed in the bag, perfection in seed sizes, and perfection in detassling. More-senior managers have measures based more on earnings growth.

Each year, Pioneer Hi-Bred employees participate directly in the success of the company through the profit-sharing program. Eligible employees share equally with their coworkers regardless of their base pay, their work location, or their job. The amount is determined by two factors—pretax profit and the number of employees participating in the program.

How Investors and Analysts View the Company

About 55 percent of Pioneer Hi-Bred's stock is held by institutional investors, and a significant portion is held by the company's founding families. Only a small percent of investors hold the stock for short-term returns.

Pioneer Hi-Bred talks to analysts who have been following the company for some time, and also to people not as familiar with the company who have been attracted by its performance over the past five years. Dollison thinks that the analysts who are familiar with Pioneer Hi-Bred have reasonably good performance models. He says, "We try to give them the information we can about what we're doing. They can use their models to predict what the results will be. We bring them up to date and help them keep within a range of possibilities." The company is spending more time with the newer analysts to make sure they understand the business. Dollison believes that most of the analysts who follow the company have a good sense of what drives the business and what the likely outcomes are, at least in the short run. Although analysts seem to be looking at cash flow more than they used to, he hears them talk most consistently about ROE and growth. He thinks the models they use—which include assumptions about acreage, sales prices, market share, and cost of sales—are somewhat influenced by Pioneer Hi-Bred's historical pattern of returns and growth. Growth is a heavy factor in the analysts' determination of a price-earnings multiple. Historically, Pioneer Hi-Bred's earnings and cash flow have been erratic following agricultural, feed grain, economic, and weather patterns. But its earnings and cash flow tend to even out over time, so earnings are a reasonable proxy for cash flow if an analyst wants to do a discounted cash-flow analysis at an assumed growth rate. Accounting and capital structure are consistent from year to year, which facilitates long-term projections and valuations.

People Interviewed

Jeffrey A. Austin, Director—Corporate Finance
Ann Bublitz, Marketing Director and Technologies Specialist
Dwight G. Dollison, Vice President and Treasurer
Brian G. Hart, Vice President and Corporate Controller
Paul W. Matson, Director of Finance—Research & Product
    Development
Paul E. Schickler, Corporate Vice President—Director, Resource
    Planning

17

Simon Property Group, Inc.

Simon, based in Indianapolis, is one of the largest publicly traded real estate investment trusts (REITs) and one of the largest owners and developers of shopping malls in the United States.[1] The company's portfolio consists of 122 retail properties operating in 28 states. These properties encompass 62 million square feet, of which approximately 37 million is company owned, include 62 regional malls, 55 community centers, 2 specialty retail centers, and 3 mixed-use projects. Regional malls contain two or more large department stores as anchor tenants and a variety of smaller stores located in enclosed promenades connecting the anchors. Community shopping centers are anchored by supermarkets, drugstores, and discount retailers.

The company was founded in the 1960s by Melvin and Herbert Simon, the current co-chairmen, and went public in 1993. David Simon, President and CEO, leads a relatively young management team with a diversity of experience from Simon and other companies. Simon is regarded for having more of the management characteristics of a publicly held company than most other REITs, and its evolution from a private to a publicly held company is a sign of changing times. The firm's transition provides a model for others to follow.

Simon was among the first fully integrated developers, owners, and managers of shopping malls with internal functions that include development, architecture, construction, engineering, management, real estate tax management, leasing, collections, finance, accounting, budgeting, market research, and legal. The firm's business success is based on its ability to

---

[1]Subsequent to interviews for this case study, Simon merged with the DeBartolo Realty Corporation to become Simon DeBartolo Group, Inc.

181

identify strong locations for shopping malls, build attractive facilities, and attract and retain a good mix of tenants. All of these factors ultimately attract shoppers to its centers. Locations for malls are selected based on demographic information for areas within 3, 5, and 10 miles. Such information includes median household income, household density, projected household growth, and existing mall and other retail facilities.

Nationwide retail chains are among Simon's best mall clients. A mall location helps these clients maximize their sales performance by (1) attracting other synergistic tenants, including movie theaters and restaurants and (2) minimizing their occupancy expense as a percentage of sales.

Each mall is run by a management team of three people responsible for leasing, property management, and development. Team members report to regional vice presidents responsible for their respective functions. The leasing manager leases space and maintains the appropriate merchandise mix. The property manager is responsible for marketing and maintaining the overall environment of the center. The development manager is responsible for expansion, department store relations, and significant remerchandising activities which could include de-leasing (paying a tenant to vacate its premises prior to the scheduled lease expiration in order to reconfigure and remerchandise the space on a more profitable basis).

John Neutzling, Executive Vice President—Management, says,

> Leasing determines cash flow. You do not run a business like this by just containing costs. Perhaps more important, leasing determines the merchandise mix, the fabric of the property, and how people respond to it compared to the competition. There are a tremendous number of shopping alternatives in this country, and there is little customer loyalty. People are going to shop in our malls if we're conveniently located, offer a comfortable, secure environment, and have a more attractive selection than our competitors.

Neutzling explains that a leasing person's objective is to do business with retailers with the greatest productivity potential. Successful retailers such as The Gap, Cachet, or The Body Shop are not only reliable from a credit perspective, but they draw shoppers who are likely to shop in other stores as well. Consequently, they frequently influence other tenants' decisions to come to a mall.

Simon has been a leader in merging shopping and entertainment. Attractive stores, restaurants, and movies all encourage people to spend time in the malls. Jerry Garvey, Executive Vice President of Development says, "If you get their time, you get their money." At a time when specialty store shopping centers without department store anchors were an unproven concept, Simon developed The Forum Shops at Caesar's, a group of high-priced retail stores attached to Caesar's Palace in Las Vegas. Because of the Las Vegas tourist trade, every few days the shops get a new market of customers with a high propensity to spend. Annual sales at the center are above $1,200 per square foot compared to the national average of $250.

Neutzling says, "We are in the business of providing our tenants with distribution channels to our shoppers. We are a conduit." He cites a large customer such as The Limited, whose stores include Limited Source, Limited Express, Cacique, Victoria's Secret, Bath and Body, Structure, Lerner, Lane Bryant, and Abercrombie & Fitch. To achieve its future growth goals, The Limited is looking at which of its own stores is most profitable nationwide, and which locations are most successful. Simon's head of leasing can sit down with The Limited's head of real estate and value ways they can achieve their growth strategy nationally. Locations where some Limited stores already are doing well are good candidates for other Limited stores.

Operating Measures

Simon's growth and profitability are based on its ability to maintain high occupancy in its malls, to develop an environment capable of producing high sales performance, to get the highest possible rent on new leases, and to keep costs under control. Often the company shares in the sales success of its tenants, charging either percentage rent based on the tenant's sales or overage rent based on sales above a defined amount.

The most important direct operating measures of an individual mall are percentage occupancy, rent per square foot, spread between rent paid by departing tenants and new tenants, and tenant sales productivity.

Specific sales measures include tenants' sales per square foot and tenants' total rental expense as a percentage of sales. Simon is the lowest of the public company mall operators, with 10.9 percent average rental expense as a percentage of sales. Simon is reimbursed for most of its direct expenses in running a mall. If those expenses become too high, however, it will lose its competitive position as a low-cost provider, or may not be able to increase rents to tenants.

Financial Performance Measures

The principal financial measures for REITs are funds from operations (FFO), EBITDA, and funds available for distribution (FAD). The principal measure of an REIT for valuation purposes is FFO; this measure is unique to the real estate industry. REIT stocks are valued and compared by multiples of FFO. Recently, Simon's stock has traded between 10.3 and 10.7 times FFO. A peer group of a dozen REITs shows current multiples ranging from 7.8 to 10.8.

FFO is defined as net income from operating activities before considering the impact of depreciation and amortization of assets that are defined as unique to real estate. (Examples of assets not unique to real estate include computers, vehicles, and capitalized financing expenses.) While not the same as cash flow, FFO provides an appropriate gauge of operating performance. (FFO is cash flow based on the average rate paid by a tenant for the entire lease; cash flow is based on what the tenant actually pays, which is typically stepped up over the lease term.)

Dennis Cavanagh, Senior Vice President of Financial Services, believes that FFO is roughly comparable to net income for a non-real-estate company. Net income for a real estate company suffers in comparison with other companies because a real estate company is very capital intensive, incurring heavy depreciation and amortization expense. Yet, well maintained, a mall typically appreciates over time. FFO provides a better measure with which to assess a company's dividend paying capability.

EBITDA is also an important financial measure used to compare REITs. EBITDA is an industry standard that measures operating performance before the effect of capital structure.

EBITDA divided by total revenue equals the operating profit margin. This industry standard measures operating efficiency, or the portion of the revenue base that the company carries to the bottom line.

Operating margins typically run in the 60 percent range for regional malls. They are relatively high because mall leases generally allow for the recovery of most operating expenses from the tenants. In addition, the capital intensive nature of real estate requires a high operating margin. Simon's operating margin exceeds 61 percent and has grown consistently since 1988.

Another measure—funds available for distribution (FAD)—is calculated by subtracting operational capital expenditures from FFO. The company's dividend divided by this number is referred to as the dividend payout ratio, a commonly used industry standard indicating the percentage of cash flow paid out in dividends and reciprocally, the amount reinvested in the company.

To retain its REIT status, Simon is required to pay out 95 percent of its taxable income as dividends. Taxable income is calculated after depreciation, so this requirement allows the company plenty of latitude in determining its dividend payout ratio. Simon currently pays out 88 percent of its FFO in dividends. Publicly held REITs in its peer group pay between 57 percent and 106 percent of FFO.

Creditworthiness Measures

When credit-rating agencies look at an REIT like Simon, they are interested in FFO growth, the company's access to capital, its existing debt structure, whether the company is willing to issue equity periodically, and how receptive the market is to the company's stock offerings. The rating agencies' quantitative measures include debt as a percentage of total market capitalization, interest coverage, and unencumbered assets. In many industries, analysts have traditionally compared book debt to book capitalization. That approach would be particularly unrealistic in this industry because of the appreciating nature of real estate. Using unencumbered assets—property with no liens—as a measure can seem somewhat restrictive to Simon because many of its assets that are encumbered have substantial interest coverage and loans less than 50 percent of property values.

Investors' Objectives

Simon investors are roughly 50 percent retail and 50 percent institutional. Many of Simon's and other REITs' shareholders are primarily motivated by yield. REITs typically compete with bonds and utility stocks for investment dollars. Simon currently pays investors a dividend yield of about 8 percent.

Long-term Strategy

Steve Sterrett, Vice President and Treasurer, would like to see Simon and its stock become a little more growth oriented. Retained earnings is Simon's cheapest source of capital. If the company could grow FFO at 8 percent per year and grow its dividend payout to 3 or 4 percent annually, it could retain an additional $10 million per year.

Sterrett sees substantial future consolidation in the industry. Simon, which has a market capitalization of $4.5 billion and manages 75 million square feet of space, is the largest REIT and mall operator in the United States, but has only a 3 percent market share of regional malls. Sterrett could see Simon growing its market share by acquiring other real estate portfolios or companies. Eliminating duplicate staff in acquired companies could cut costs substantially. Sterrett thinks that Simon will have a number of opportunities to acquire new properties for at least two reasons: First, a large part of the industry consists of private companies that own two or three malls. When the owners want to sell for estate liquidity or other reasons, a large REIT like Simon is a logical buyer. Second, some insurance companies and other institutional investors that have acted as direct real estate owners or lenders in the past would prefer to reduce their own overhead and invest in real estate through an equity position in an REIT.

Project Feasibility Studies

When Simon does a feasibility study for a new mall, it projects annual EBIDTA and FFO, typically for the fourth year, compared with cash invested. If the cash-flow stream fluctuates significantly, IRR may be used.

The investment amount for a new regional mall typically ranges from $100 million to $200 million. In a typical project, Simon might spend $100,000 on an initial feasibility study. Based upon this initial effort, additional funding may be authorized to further explore the project. Once feasibility is determined, the company pursues a preliminary commitment from lenders as well as anchor tenants and starts pre-leasing other spaces. Simon uses an internal project approval form that documents the project and the underlying critical assumptions, major tenants, timing of construction, and the major risks. Though Cavanagh shares the corporate aversion to creating more committees, he supports the practice of an interdisciplinary committee sharing the responsibility for approving large projects.

Incentive Compensation

About 500 people in headquarters, regional offices, and malls participate in incentive compensation plans. Those plans have been redesigned over the past two years. Simon has designed a performance measurement system for its home office and field organizations that focuses on the results expected by shareholders. It has developed a matrix to determine incentive compensation for the vice presidents of management, leasing, and development in each region. The matrix defines the percentage of a person's cash bonus that is determined by each measure. The measures include FFO and percentage occupancy goals for the corporation, and FFO, minimum rent, percentage occupancy, and specialty leasing income goals for the region. Other measures include tenant allowance goals for leasing vice presidents, redevelopment and portfolio enhancement goals for development vice presidents, and cost control goals for property management vice presidents. The goals are determined by the vice presidents and other senior officers of the company in the course of establishing the annual budget and are monitored through monthly reporting and quarterly portfolio review meetings. Though some of the specific goals differ by function, the system is designed to strongly encourage the functions to work together to share the performance of their respective portfolios.

There are 18 people above the regional level on Simon's management committee. A significant portion of the annual cash bonus for each of these individuals is derived from corporate FFO. Fifty-two people, including all vice presidents and above, participate in a restricted stock incentive plan which is based on FFO performance over a five-year period, with vesting occurring over nine years.

There is also an MBO plan for staff in the administrative areas, which includes financial services, architecture, construction, and legal. A metric for a person in the finance function might relate to how promptly tenant rent is collected. A tenant coordinator in a mall may be evaluated on timeliness of tenant openings. The measure for a legal person is the turnaround time for leasing and closing documents. Management and people skills are discussed in performance evaluations and influence the annual raise determination but have no bearing on the amount of bonuses.

The Role of the Finance Function

The financial services group mission is consistent with the company's mission statement to become the dominant developer and manager of real estate in North America and to increase shareholder value by focusing on enhanced financial performance and organizational professionalism. The service orientation of the finance function is an important part of its mission statement. Finance people are encouraged not to be just number crunchers, but to help managers in the regions and the malls understand the numbers. Action guidelines in the financial services group mission statement include the following:

□ Focus on maximizing Simon's earnings, FFO, and cash flow.

□ Maintain a responsive customer orientation by providing financial information and tools to Simon's managers and others to facilitate their understanding of business performance, issues, and opportunities.

□ Produce management and compliance reporting that is timely and accurate and also insightful in its business perspective, focusing not only on historic performance but also on future implications.

□ Maintain a sense of independence in capturing, evaluating, and reporting on business activities.

□ Help to continually improve the effectiveness of the systems environment.

□ Ensure that the organization, staff, systems, practices, and controls support Simon's growth strategy.

Executive Information System

The finance function provides each region with a monthly report that shows key performance measures and results. Simon's executive information systems give regional and mall managers the information they need in a way that is not intimidating. They provide relatively easy access to all critical performance measures. The executive information systems are part of a strategic systems plan designed to provide an information base that supports strategic and tactical decision making and meets format, availability, security, and integrity requirements in a cost-effective manner.

People Interviewed

Dennis Cavanagh, Senior Vice President—Financial Services
John R. Neutzling, Executive Vice President—Management
John Rulli, Senior Vice President—Human Resources & Corporate
    Operations
Stephen E. Sterrett, Vice President & Treasurer

Appendices

A
Survey Results

A mail survey was sent to FEI members at 450 companies in the United States and Canada; 153 responses (34 percent) were received from companies in a broad range of industries. The purpose of the mail survey was to validate the interview findings from the 12 case-study companies across a larger number of companies. The questions were designed to have clear-cut answers suitable for tabulation. Most of the questions were multiple-choice; some called for brief written responses. A tabulation of responses to the multiple-choice questions and a summary of written responses are found below. Industries of the survey respondents are listed in Appendix B.

1. Which of the following do you believe has a stronger effect on your company's share price?

	Percentage of Total Respondents
Net income	47.1
Free cash flow	45.8
Did not answer	7.1

2. What quantitative financial measures do you use for performance measurement and compensation? Please check all that apply:

	Percentage of Total Respondents
Earnings-Based Measures	
Operating earnings	72.5
Return on common equity	34.6
Return on net assets	32.7

Return on investment	26.8
Economic value added	26.1
Return on assets	21.6

Cash-Flow-Based Measures
Total shareholder return	29.4
Cash flow return on investment	20.9

Other Measures
Market value added	8.5

Respondents were asked to specify other performance measures they use. Following are the measures they listed:

Earnings-Based Measures
Revenue growth
Net income
Pretax income improvement
Earnings per share
Earnings before interest and taxes
Return on capital
Return on total capital employed
Operating income return on capital employed compared to a benchmark
Return on average capital employed
Return on invested capital
Return on required capital
Return on operating assets
Return on sales
Return on revenue (bank holding company)
Operating return on investment
Reduction in operating costs

Cash-Flow-Based Measures
Cash flow
Discounted cash flow
Earnings before interest, income taxes, depreciation, and amortization
Free cash flow
Growth in free cash flow
Cash from operations

Cash flow after investments
Net funds flow
Cash return on net assets

Other Measures
Growth
Working capital performance
Inventory turnover
Market share performance
Share price versus peers
Various nonfinancial strategic goals

3. For what percentage of your workforce is compensation tied in some way to financial performance measures?

	Percentage of Total Respondents
Average	41.5
Median	15.0
0%	0.8
1 to 3%	11.8
4 to 5%	13.1
6 to 10%	15.0
11 to 25%	13.7
26 to 50%	7.8
51 to 75%	3.3
76 to 99%	9.7
100%	22.2
Did not answer	2.6

4. How do you calculate total capital invested in a business unit for performance measurement purposes? Please check one:

	Percentage of Total Respondents
Book stockholder equity plus debt	26.8
Historical capital invested	25.5
Book stockholder equity	5.9
Did not specify	41.8

Other methods explained included the following:

☐ Total assets minus non-interest-bearing liabilities.

☐ Total assets minus current liabilities; both exclude cash and financing items.

☐ Net assets minus non-interest-bearing liabilities.

☐ Total assets at depreciation replacement value minus operating liabilities other than debt.

☐ Historical net fixed assets plus accounts receivable, inventory, and other assets.

☐ Historical capital invested less non-interest-bearing liabilities, adjusted for known impairments in value.

☐ Current assets (excluding cash) plus gross fixed assets plus other assets minus current liabilities (excluding debt) minus deferred taxes minus other liabilities (excluding debt).

☐ Total assets (book basis) less non-interest-bearing current liabilities. Goodwill is not amortized and for the most part inventory is reflected at current value (i.e., we add back LIFO reserves).

☐ Total assets plus LIFO reserves, interest-bearing short-term liabilities, accrued income taxes, capitalized value of leases minus interest-bearing short-term investments and short-term liabilities.

☐ Some assets at historical cost and some marked to market at current value.

☐ Required capital determined by riskiness of product line.

☐ Assign capital based on various forms of risk including credit, interest rate, operational, business, and disruption.

☐ Required capital under regulatory standards as a proxy for capital at risk.

☐ Intrinsic value of business units determined based on net present value of future cash flows. Reasonable capital structures determined based on those intrinsic values for internal performance measurement purposes.

☐ Discounted cash flow, our primary measure, is future focused; hence invested capital is a point of reference only.

☐ We are one business unit and our key issue is R&D project resource allocation, where we look at incremental capital.

☐ Total capital invested not applicable because we are currently a development company.

5. What adjustments, if any, do you make to your performance measures for capital invested in a business unit?

	Percentage of Respondents Who Answered Question	Percentage of Total Respondents
Capitalized operating leases	47.6	19.6
LIFO reserves	25.4	10.5
Deferred taxes	25.4	10.5
Cumulative goodwill amortization	23.8	9.8
Addition of unrecorded goodwill	20.6	8.5
Current value of property, plant, and equipment	15.9	6.5
Bad debt reserves	12.7	5.2
Warranty reserves/liabilities	6.3	2.6
Question not answered		58.2

Other adjustments explained included the following:

☐ Adjust for intercompany borrowings.

☐ Remove goodwill and intangibles.

☐ Remove or add capital (undiscounted free cash flow) to bring product line to required capital levels.

☐ Employ return on total capital computed with and without goodwill amortization.

☐ Make no adjustments to balance sheets of individual units except to remove items that may reside on their balance sheets for legal or tax purposes but for which they do not have operating responsibility.

☐ Add to net assets imputed goodwill in those business units in which acquisitions have been completed on a pooling basis.

□ Do not use cash taxes in NOPAT calculation, but push down deferred taxes to business units in capital calculation.

□ Adjust for unusual write-offs such as restructuring charges.

□ Eliminate foreign currency translation adjustments and unrealized gains and losses from marking investments to fair value.

6. To the extent you adjust your performance measures for total capital invested for specific balance sheet items such as those cited above, do you make corresponding adjustments to your earnings measure?

	Percentage of Respondents Who Answered Question	Percentage of Total Respondents
Yes	65.0	26.1
No	35.0	14.4

7. When calculating total capital invested in your business units for performance measurement purposes, do you include any of the following intangible expenses that cannot be capitalized under current accounting rules?

	Percentage of Total Respondents
R&D	2.6
Training	2.0
Other intangibles	2.6

8. How do you determine your discount rate for capital budgeting?

	Percentage of Total Respondents
WACC	35.3
CAPM	5.9

Other methods mentioned by respondents include the following:

□ Country- or region-specific cost of capital.

□ Internal borrowing rate based on current working capital revolver loan.

☐ Long-term borrowing rate.

☐ Risk adjusted for equivalent stage of project (biotechnology company).

☐ Target ROE (bank).

☐ IRR compared to the cost of capital.

☐ For acquisitions at business unit level, 75 basis points above the commercial paper rate.

☐ Benchmark ROI for corporation against competing public companies; this rolled up into RONA for operating units.

☐ Expectation of members'/owners' returns (dairy cooperative).

☐ ROI with *beta* for oil companies.

9. Do you use different discount rates for different business activities or investment opportunities?

	Percentage of Total Respondents
Yes	46.4
No	49.0
Did not answer	4.6

10. Does your capital budgeting analysis include investments in asset options or real options–investments in future opportunities that may or may not materialize?

	Percentage of Total Respondents
Yes	21.6
No	74.5
Did not answer	3.9

11. Does your capital budgeting analysis include investments in intangibles such as training and R&D?

	Percentage of Total Respondents
Yes	37.9
No	60.8
Did not answer	1.3

12. Does your capital budgeting analysis include decision trees, multiple possible outcomes, or other forms of probability analysis?

	Percentage of Total Respondents
Yes	40.5
No	57.5
Did not answer	2.0

B

Survey Respondents by Industry

Aerospace	3
Airlines	2
Apparel	2
Beverages	3
Building Materials, Glass	1
Chemicals	7
Commercial Banks	5
Computer and Data Services	3
Computers, Office Equipment	6
Diversified Financials	2
Electric and Gas Utilities	2
Electronics, Electrical Equipment	14
Engineering, Construction	2
Entertainment	2
Food	6
Food Services	2
Forest and Paper Products	2
Furniture	2
General Merchandisers	3
Health Care	1
Industrial and Farm Equipment	6
Insurance	3
Metal Products	3
Metals	9
Mining, Crude-Oil Production	4

Motor Vehicles and Parts	4
Office Supplies	2
Petroleum Refining	8
Pharmaceuticals	7
Pipelines	2
Publishing, Printing	3
Railroads	2
Scientific, Photo, Control Equipment	8
Soaps, Cosmetics	2
Specialist Retailers	3
Telecommunications	6
Temporary Help	1
Textiles	3
Tobacco	1
Toys, Sporting Goods	1
Transportation Equipment	1
Waste Management	1
Wholesalers	2
Anonymous	1

C

Interview Protocol

The following protocol was used for on-site interviews of the 12 case-study companies.

1. What types of financial performance measures do you use?
    a. Do you use traditional accounting-based performance measures such as growth in sales and earnings, return on sales, and return on investment?
    b. Do you use cash flow return on investment?
    c. Do you use economic profit, also known as economic value added? Do you use market value added?

2. What do you believe your investors' objectives are in holding your company's stock? Price appreciation? Steady dividends? Some combination of the two?

3. How do you correlate cash flow return on investment, economic profit, or other measures you may use to the value of your company's stock? Do you have any reason to believe that investors and security analysts think differently? Have you explained publicly the internal performance measures you use?

4. In what way do you use cash-flow-based, economic-profit, or other measures related to shareholder value creation to measure the performance of your business units and business managers?
    a. What types of financial and nonfinancial performance measures or value drivers are used?
    b. How are the performance measures you use for your business units adapted for performance measurement of business

managers? Are they adapted to conform to a given manager's scope of responsibility and job objectives?

c.　To what extent are these measures used for overall performance appraisal or for actual dollar compensation of business managers?

d.　For how many levels of management in a given business unit is performance appraisal and/or compensation tied to such measures?

e.　Can you cite examples of how managers have used cash-flow-based, economic profit, or similar performance measures to make strategic decisions to improve your company's performance? (Examples of strategic decisions might include investing in new projects, divesting business units, or disposal of assets.)

f.　How has the use of measures related to shareholder value creation changed the behavior of your managers and the culture of your organization?

5.　How does the finance function work with line business units to develop performance measures? How have you educated your employees in the use of these measures?

6.　Has your performance measurement system caused you to increase your delegation of decision making and spending authority to managers at various levels?

7.　How did you decide on the measures you use? To the extent that you compared different types of measures such as economic profit or cash flow return on investment, what did you find the principal advantages and disadvantages to be?

8.　What problems have you encountered implementing these measures? Have you had any difficulty dividing your company into business units or profit centers for performance measurement purposes?

9.　What types of internal financial reporting systems have you developed to track your performance measures on a continuing basis?

10. How do you calculate the amount of capital invested in each of your businesses?

    a. Does the amount include investments in intangibles such as training and research and development?

    b. Do you make other adjustments such as the current cost of capital equipment?

    c. How do you adjust the amount of capital invested for disposal of assets?

11. How do you calculate the cost of capital for your business units?

    a. Do you use the weighted average cost of capital for the company?

    b. Do you use different capital costs for different business units?

12. Has your performance measurement system caused you to re-examine your company's capital structure and your thoughts about debt capacity and leverage?

13. To what degree is your management of financial risks (interest rate, foreign exchange, commodity price, and equity price risks) oriented toward the company's long-term projected cash flow and valuation of the company?

14. To what degree do you believe there is a potential conflict in your company between managing for quarterly net income and earnings per share and cash flow over a longer term? An example of a conflict might be a project with a high overall return that will depress earnings per share in the short term. If there is a potential conflict, what is your company's way of resolving it?

15. How do you make your capital budgeting decisions?

    a. What is your company's procedure for submitting, discussing, and deciding on proposals? What people from finance and other functions are involved?

    b. How are various financial and nonfinancial considerations taken into account when you prioritize projects that meet the company's return criteria?

    c. Please comment briefly on your use of payback periods, net present value, and internal rate of return; the discount rates or hurdle rates you use; how discount rates used vary among business units and projects; and adjustments you make for factors such as project risks, project synergies, and learning curves.

d. Does your capital budgeting analysis include asset options or real options?

e. Does your capital budgeting analysis include investments in intangibles such as knowledge creation and research and development that cannot be capitalized under current accounting rules?

f. To what degree are your capital budgeting methods coordinated with your cash-flow-based or economic-profit performance measures?

16. Could you help us develop a few easy-to-understand numerical examples of how you use financial performance measures, how you calculate appropriate measures for each business unit, and how you make your capital budgeting decisions? (We are interested in the analytic and measurement techniques you use, not in any financial information you prefer to keep confidential. We are willing to work with hypothetical situations and numbers.)

Bibliography

Copeland, Tom, Tim Koller, and Jack Murrin. *Valuation: Measuring and Managing the Value of Companies*. New York: Wiley, 1994.

The authors describe what is required to become a value manager. The value manager must focus on long-run cash-flow returns, not quarter-to-quarter changes in EPS, and must view businesses dispassionately as investments in productive capacity that do or do not earn returns above their opportunity costs of capital. The authors compare the DCF and economic profit models. They recommend a way to analyze historical performance to lay the groundwork for estimating future cash flows; how to forecast company performance, line item by line item; how to estimate the cost of capital; and how to estimate continuing value. The book also recommends ways to value multi-business companies, companies with foreign currency cash flows, and companies outside the United States. The authors caution that mergers and acquisitions have a high failure rate, often because the acquiror pays too much, and they recommend steps for a successful merger and acquisition program. A chapter on using option pricing shows how to value asset and liability options. It provides examples where asset or liability options have identifiable value for companies in the pharmaceutical, oil, and mining industries.

McTaggart, James M., Peter W. Kontes, and Michael C. Mankins. *The Value Imperative*. New York: Free Press, 1994.

The authors start with the premise that most companies inherently possess an enormous potential to increase value for their shareholders. Specifically, companies must develop value-based management systems that align the objectives of their entire organizations with strategies tied to the creation of shareholder value. Furthermore, they must deal systematically with external forces such as competition and internal forces such as institutional inertia. They also must build five key processes that are institutional value drivers: governance (roles and responsibilities of the board, management, shareholders, and other stakeholders in managing the legal relationship between the corporation, shareholders, and other stakeholders), strategic planning, resource allocation, performance management, and top management compensation. Many companies have failed to achieve superior performance because they have not linked these processes. The authors discuss the strategic determinants of value creation: market economics, competitive position, and financial determinants. They explain that ROE and equity growth over time determine the stream of equity cash flow, and therefore determine the warranted value of a company or business unit. **Warranted equity value** is based on management's own best estimate of the future equity cash flow discounted at the cost of equity capital. The authors believe that economic profit is the best single-period measure for companies and their business units, but should never be used for strategic investment decisions. The best way to ensure that a proposed investment will create value is to compare the value of the business with and without that proposed investment.

New Corporate Performance Measures: A Research Report. New York: The Conference Board, 1995.

Traditional accounting and financial measures were developed to meet regulatory and financial reporting requirements rather than to run businesses. They are too historical, lack predictive power, do not capture key business changes until it is too late, and give inadequate consideration to difficult-to-quantify resources such as intellectual capital. New performance measures are intended to augment traditional financial measures and provide a more comprehensive management tool to enhance the corporation's performance. They serve as leading indicators of financial performance. Examples include quality of output, customer satisfaction/retention, employee turnover, employee training, R&D investments, R&D productivity, new product development, market growth/success, and environmental competitiveness. Performance measurement processes should be initiated by top management and then managers and employees should buy in. In designing new performance measures, companies sometimes start by temporarily disregarding all the measures they have used in the past. Measures should be tied to the strategic vision of the company, and changed as goals are met and new priorities are defined. Some companies do not disclose their key internal performance measures because they are still inconsistent and need further development, and also because disclosing those measures could reduce their competitive advantage. Case-study companies believe there is a link between key performance measures and the bottom line even though it is difficult to quantify.

Rappaport, Alfred. *Creating $hareholder Value*. New York: Free Press, 1986.

Rappaport discusses the weaknesses of accounting-based measures such as EPS, ROI, and ROE. He describes the valuation of a company based on estimated cash flows, the cost of capital, and a residual value. He shows how value drivers such as the sales growth rate, the operating profit margin, the income tax rate, working capital investment, fixed capital investment, and the forecast duration are incorporated into share-holder value calculations. The perpetuity method for calculating residual value is described. Rappaport explains how the stock market sends signals to management: the current stock price is an indication of whether the market expects the company to earn at a rate above its cost of capital. The author describes executive performance measurement and compensation plans based on value creation. He recommends ways to value growth strategies at both the corporate and business-unit level. For acquisitions, the book describes a financial evaluation process that involves both a self-evaluation by the acquiring company and the evaluation of the target company.

Roussel, Philip A., Kamal N. Saad, and Tamara J. Erickson. *Third Generation R&D: Managing the Link to Corporate Strategy*. Cambridge, Mass.: Harvard Business School Press, 1991.

As our economy becomes more knowledge- and technology-based, intangibles such as R&D become more important drivers of shareholder value. The authors describe first generation R&D, where research is treated as an overhead cost, second generation R&D, where management recognizes the project nature of R&D and seeks to quantify the costs and benefits of individual projects, and third generation R&D, where general managers and R&D managers work together as partners, making decisions together on how research relates to product planning and long-term strategic planning. Methods are recommended for approving and managing a portfolio of R&D projects. Matrixes are shown in which companies compare the level of risk to the potential reward and the expected reward to the probability of technical success for portfolios of R&D projects. Because of the uncertainty of future cash flows related to R&D projects, NPV analysis plays only a small role in the methods recommended for budgeting, prioritizing, and approving R&D expenditures.

Stewart, G. Bennett, III. *The Quest for Value.* New York: Harper Collins, 1991.

This is the most detailed book available on the economic-value-added metric. Stewart argues that earnings, EPS, and earnings growth are misleading measures of corporate performance, and explains why returns above the cost of capital are better indicators of value creation. He advocates a method to calculate NOPAT and capital invested in a business. He recommends numerous adjustments to both earnings and capital to remove accounting distortions and create an accurate measure of economic profit. Book depreciation is replaced with economic depreciation. Equity equivalents such as deferred tax reserves, LIFO reserves, and cumulative goodwill amortization are added to book capital to compute a more realistic value for economic capital; corresponding adjustments are made to earnings. Stewart shows how economic value added has predicted the market value added (the difference between market value and cash invested) for the largest companies in the United States. He provides case studies and recommendations to management on implementing economic value added.

Glossary

Asset Option Asset options, also known as real options, include options to expand, contract, or defer projects, and investments in future opportunities that may or may not materialize. For example, an investment in R&D or in a feasibility study might lead to another decision a year from now to either abandon the project or to make an additional investment. Decision trees might be used in this type of capital budgeting analysis.

Beta See Capital Asset Pricing Model.

Break-up Value A value of a company based on summing up the value of its component parts. An investor may believe that one or more subsidiaries of a company would be valued differently if it were independent.

Capital Asset Pricing Model (CAPM) A model for calculating the cost of equity capital. The formula is:

$$\text{Cost of equity} = \text{Current risk-free rate} + (beta \times \text{market risk premium for common stocks})$$

The risk-free rate, as its name implies, is the return available from an investment that carries no risk. In practice, Treasury bill rates are used as a proxy for the risk-free rate. Some companies consider a longer-term Treasury bond rate to be a more appropriate risk-free rate to compare with the cost of equity.

Beta is a measure of the risk of a particular stock compared to the stock market as a whole. It is the covariance of the stock with the market. It is derived by running a regression analysis between the returns on a specific stock and those of a broad index of stocks such as the Standard and Poor's 500. A stock with a *beta* of more than one has greater volatility than the underlying market, and vice versa. The CAPM states that the expected risk premium for a given stock is proportional to its *beta*. The accuracy of *beta*s for particular company stocks has been questioned in recent years.

The market risk premium is the incremental rate of return required by investors to hold a well-diversified portfolio of stocks rather than risk-free securities. The historical difference between the stock market return and the risk-free rate, used in the formula above, can be found in the frequently used yearbook *Stocks, Bonds, Bills and Inflation*, by Ibbotson Associates of Chicago. According to the 1995 yearbook, the arithmetic-mean difference between the return for large-company stocks and U.S. Treasury bills between 1926 and 1994 was 8.5 percent. For the same period, the difference between the large-company stock return and the long-term government bond return was 7 percent. There is an additional risk premium for small companies.

By necessity, this method of valuation is judgmental. The company's management, securities analysts, and lenders will inevitably have a variety of different conclusions based on different assumptions about future earnings.

Capital Budgeting A process of ranking projects and deciding which ones to invest in. Companies often use quantitative methods such as NPV, IRR, and payback to evaluate and rank prospective projects but consider many nonquantitative factors as well.

Capital Invested For performance measurement purposes, the total capital invested in the company or one of its business units is often considered to be book capital or actual cash invested, with some adjustment for divestitures. Some companies define capital invested as net assets, which is total assets minus nonfinancial liabilities.

Cash-Flow-Based Performance Measures Performance measures based on free cash flow or other cash-flow-based figures.

Cash Flow Return on Investment (CFROI) Cash flow generated as a percentage of cash invested in the business. Cash flow generated is often considered to be free cash flow (see glossary definition). Cash invested in the business is often considered to be total assets minus current libilities. A more specific, proprietary model compares the cumulative cash invested in a business with the cash it is currently producing, recognizing that there is a finite life over which depreciating assets will produce cash and a residual value to nondepreciating assets such as working capital and land. When that model is used for valuation, assumptions are made about a growth in invested capital funded by free cash flow and a fade of above-average cash flow returns to market averages over time.

Cost of Capital See Weighted Average Cost of Capital.

Decision Tree A method for analyzing a series of decisions and events or possible outcomes. Probabilities may be assigned to possible outcomes and expected values may be calculated.

Discount Rate The rate used to discount future cash flows back to a present value. In corporate valuation, the WACC is normally used. Some companies adjust discount rates for different businesses or projects based on estimated risk for valuation or investment analysis purposes. For example, sometimes the discount rate used for a subsidiary is a representative weighted average cost of capital for independent companies in the subsidiary's business.

Discounted Cash Flow (DCF) The present value of future cash flows. Discounted cash flow analysis is used in corporate valuation and in capital budgeting.

Discounted Payback The time until a project has a positive NPV.

Duration Duration has several meanings in finance. In the context of this study, it is the point in time in a company's planning horizon after which returns are not expected to exceed the cost of capital.

Earnings-Based Performance Measures Performance measures based on net income or other accrual-based figures.

Earnings Before Interest, Income Taxes, Depreciation, and Amortization (EBITDA) A frequently used measure of a company's cash flow and ability to service debt.

Economic Profit See Economic Value Added.

Economic Value Added Net operating profit after taxes (NOPAT) minus a capital charge, which is calculated as the WACC times the amount of capital invested. Also referred to as Economic Profit. See Net Operating Profit After Taxes and Economic Profit.

Free Cash Flow The cash flow amount for a given year used in discounted cash flow valuations of companies. It is cash left from operating income before deducting noncash charges such as depreciation and amortization, but after deducting payment of taxes and incremental investment in equipment and working capital that are required to sustain the business. The formula for calculation of free cash flow is net income plus depreciation and other noncash deductions plus after-tax interest minus the estimated increase in working capital minus estimated capital expenditures.

Funds Available for Distribution (FAD) A frequently used financial measure for real estate investment trusts. FAD is calculated from funds from operations (see below).

Funds From Operations (FFO) A frequently used financial measure for real estate investment trusts. FFO is defined as net income from operating activities before the impact of depreciation and amortization of assets that are unique to real estate.

Growing Perpetuity A method for calculating the residual value of a business that assumes free cash flows will grow in perpetuity. The formula is:

$$\text{Present value} = \frac{\text{Cash flow} \; (1 + \text{growth rate})}{\text{Discount rate} - \text{growth rate}}$$

A company might project cash flows over a certain number of years and use a perpetuity or growing perpetuity to value cash flows beyond that time rather than trying to estimate a terminal value. For example, if a company projects cash flows for five years, it may calculate a growing perpetuity based on its projected free cash flow in year five and discount the resulting value to the present. See Perpetuity.

Hurdle Rate A minimum acceptable rate of return on a project; the discount rate used in an NPV analysis for capital budgeting. Often, it is a company's WACC. A project whose projected return exceeds the hurdle rate has a positive NPV.

Internal Rate of Return (IRR) A discount rate that, when applied to a series of projected future cash flows, would yield an NPV of zero.

Lead Steer A knowledgeable investor with a long-term orientation who leads other investors.

LIFO Reserve The difference between LIFO (last-in, first-out) and FIFO (first-in, first-out) value of inventory. It is a measure of the extent to which LIFO inventory is understated in value.

Market Value Added The change in the difference between the market and the book value of equity over a given period of time.

Momentum Investor An investor looking for near-term price movements.

Monte Carlo Simulations Simulations of multiple possible outcomes in which a computer generates a large number of values within an expected range for each variable.

Multiple Possible Outcomes A method for taking risk into account in investment decisions. Expected, best, and worst case scenarios are assumed for a number of factors relevant to a project such as growth of the market, market share, prices, and costs. Based on the variability of these factors, a range of possible outcomes for the project is calculated.

Net Operating Profit After Taxes (NOPAT) Profits from operations after taxes, but before financing costs and before noncash charges except depreciation. Depreciation is subtracted in the calculation of NOPAT because it is a true economic expense.

Net Present Value (NPV) The sum of the present values of projected cash outflows and cash inflows. A positive NPV indicates a financially attractive proposal based on the discount rate used.

Operating Margin Pretax profit before extraordinary items. Revenues minus the cost of goods sold minus selling, general, and administrative expenses.

Payback A calculation of the point in time when nominal future cash inflows cover the cost of an investment. This method has been used in capital budgeting for a long time. Its primary advantage is simplicity.

Perpetuity An investment offering a level stream of cash flows in perpetuity. A business may assume that at some point it will no longer be able to generate investment opportunities at returns above the cost of capital. In economic terms, the business will have reached a point where it is no longer producing real growth in value. Further investment will generate income, but the present value of that income will be equal to the present value of the investment. Since further investment is unwarranted, all the cash flow generated can be capitalized at the appropriate discount rate.

$$\text{Present value of perpetuity} = \frac{\text{Yearly cash flow}}{\text{Discount rate}}$$

See Growing Perpetuity.

Present Value The discounted value of a future cash flow.

Profitability Index The present value of cash inflows divided by the present value of investment outflows.

Range of Possible Outcomes See Multiple Possible Outcomes.

Real Estate Investment Trust (REIT) A company engaged in real estate investments that is able to deduct dividends paid to stockholders, substantially eliminating federal double taxation (taxation at both the corporate level and the investor level) subject to organizational requirements, income tests, asset tests, and annual distribution requirements defined in the U.S. Internal Revenue Code.

Real Option See Asset Option.

Relative Total Shareholder Return The total return, in both dividends and share price appreciation, earned by the company's shareholders in relation to the shareholder returns generated by similar companies over any given time period.

Return on Assets (ROA) Net income after taxes as a percent of total assets.

Return on Common Equity (ROE) See Return on Equity.

Return on Equity (ROE) Net income after taxes as a percent of the book value of shareholders' equity. For the purpose of this study, return on common equity is synonymous with return on equity.

Return on Investment (ROI) Net income after taxes as a percent of net book value.

Return on Net Assets (RONA) Earnings minus financing charges divided by net assets. (Net assets are total assets minus nonfinancial liabilities.)

Sensitivity Analysis The calculation of multiple scenarios (for example in a present value analysis) to show the effect of varying a given factor.

Total Shareholder Return (TSR) Change in price of company shares plus dividends reinvested. Dividends are assumed to be reinvested in the company to take earnings on dividends into account.

Value Drivers Financial and nonfinancial performance measures at various levels of an organization that are systematically linked to cash flow and the creation of shareholder value and used to evaluate managers' performance.

Warranted Equity Value An internal valuation of a business unit or entity based on management's best estimate of the future equity cash flow it will generate over time, discounted at the cost of equity capital.

Weighted Average Cost of Capital (WACC) A weighted average cost of a company's debt and equity capital that represents its aggregate after-tax cost of raising funds. The market values of debt and equity are calculated as percentages of total capitalization (market value of debt and equity). Formula:

WACC = after-tax cost of debt as a percentage
of capitalization + cost of equity ×
equity as a percentage of capitalization.
Capitalization is the sum of debt and equity.

About the Author

Henry A. Davis is an independent consultant and writer in corporate finance and banking and is a contributing editor of *International Treasurer.* He has been vice president of research and consulting at Ferguson & Co., director of research and treasurer at the Globecon Group, vice president at Bank of Boston, and assistant vice president at Bankers Trust Company. He is the co-author of *The Lender's Guide to the Knowledge Economy* (Amacom Books, 1996), *Foreign Exchange Risk Management: A Survey of Corporate Practices* (FERF, 1995), and *The Empowered Organization: Redefining the Roles and Practices of Finance* (FERF, 1994). He is the author of *Financial Products for Medium-Sized Companies* (FERF, 1989), *Electronic Data Interchange and Corporate Trade Payments* (FERF, 1988), and *Cash Management and the Payments System: Ground Rules, Costs and Risks* (FERF, 1986). Mr. Davis holds a bachelor's degree from Princeton University and an MBA from the Darden Graduate Business School at the University of Virginia.

Acknowledgments

A research project of this nature is not completed without the help of many people. I would like to thank FERF staff members for their support from the first draft of the proposal to the completion of the book: Jim Lewis for his overall guidance, Bill Sinnett for his help in every phase of the project, Janet Hastie for her editorial guidance throughout the project, and Paul Borgese for his suggestions on the proposal and the questionnaires. I also thank all of the participants in the case-study companies for their time and effort and the ideas they shared in the interviews, in follow-up discussions, and in approval of the case-study drafts. In addition, I thank the project advisory committee, including Doug Hartt, chairman; Charlie Cantwell; Paul Gifford; Arthur Neis; and John van Dyke for their help on the overall focus on the project, selection of the case-study companies, interpretation of research findings, and resolution of technical details. Finally, I would like to thank Professors Bill Sihler, Ken Eades, and Susan Chaplinski of the Darden Graduate Business School at the University of Virginia for their advice on preparing the proposal, as well as Mark Benson of CS First Boston Corporation and James Sullivan of Prudential Securities for their guidance on real estate investment trusts.

Other Titles of Interest from
Financial Executives Research Foundation, Inc.

❏ **REENGINEERING THE FINANCE FUNCTION**
The Hackett Group
Finance is at times characterized as overburdened by complex processes
and excessive controls. The vision of reengineering is one of driving
down transaction processing costs, redirecting the flow of work toward
more analysis, and giving the finance staff an expanded role in strategic
decision making. This study shows how six companies reduced costs
while strengthening the finance function. Case-study companies are
Advanced Micro Devices, Inc., Allergan, Inc., CDI Corporation, EDS,
Johnson & Johnson, and Motorola Inc.
1995, 73 pp.   **(095-03)**

❏ **INTERNAL AUDIT AND INNOVATION**
James A. F. Stoner and Frank M. Werner
Revolutionary rates of change are occurring in internal audit, providing
opportunities for audit to make increasingly important contributions to
business competitiveness. This study will show you how to reduce the
time devoted to traditional audits and then use the time saved to improve organizational effectiveness. Case-study companies are American
Standard Companies Inc., Baxter International Inc., Gulf Canada Resources Ltd., Motorola Inc., and Raychem Corp.
1995, 262 pp.   **(095-01)**

❏ **FOREIGN EXCHANGE RISK MANAGEMENT**
Henry A. Davis and Frederick C. Militello, Jr.
Senior management is aware of the complexity of exposures and the need
to understand how they are managed. Interviews with treasurers and
foreign exchange managers at 22 leading companies—including FMC
Corporation, General Electric Company, McDonald's Corporation, Merck
& Co., Inc., and Mobil Corporation—provide an insider's view of how
treasury is working with management to define business and financial
risks. Topics covered include hedging and risk management methods,
corporate policies, and accounting and regulatory issues.
1995, 175 pp.   **(094-11)**

❏ **THE EMPOWERED ORGANIZATION**
Henry A. Davis and Frederick C. Militello, Jr.
Companies can perform more successfully and more quickly, and
motivation will be higher, if both authority and responsibility are in the
hands of the people closest to the product and the customer. This study
will help you articulate your corporate values and show you how to
reconcile employee empowerment with control. Case-study companies
are CoreStates Financial Corp, Corning Incorporated, W. L. Gore and
Associates, Inc., Harley-Davidson, Inc., The Geo. E. Keith Company,
Herman Miller, Inc., Silicon Graphics, Inc., Steelcase Inc., and Levi Strauss
& Co.
1994, 228 pp.   **(094-03)**

❖ **To order call 1-800-680-FERF** ❖

3575   93